THE CHRISTMAS BOOK

THE CHRISTMAS BOOK

AUTHORS

Text by Lynn Bryan   Recipes by Jo Seagar

❖

ART DIRECTOR
Donna Hoyle

PHOTOGRAPHER
John Pettitt

❖

FLORAL DESIGNER
Fionna Hill

STYLIST
Craig Thorburn

This edition produced exclusively in the UK for WH Smith Ltd.
Greenbridge Road, Swindon SN3 3LD.

Published by Weldon Publishing
a division of Kevin Weldon & Associates Pty Ltd
372 Eastern Valley Way, Willoughby, NSW 2068, Australia

Publishing Manager: Robin Burgess
Publishing Coordinator: Donna Hoyle
Editor: Diana Harris
Designer: Donna Hoyle

First Published 1991
© Copyright: Kevin Weldon & Associates Pty Ltd 1991
© Copyright Design: Kevin Weldon & Associates Pty Ltd 1991

Typesetting: Jazz Graphics, Auckland, New Zealand
Finished Artwork: PR Graphics, Auckland, New Zealand
Printed by: Griffin Press, Adelaide, Australia

National Library of Australia Cataloguing-in-Publication Data:
Bryan, Lynn
The Christmas Book
Includes Index
ISBN 1 875410 16 3
1. Christmas. 2. Christmas decorations 3. Christmas cookery.
I. Seagar, Joanna II. Title
394 268282

All rights reserved. No part of this work covered by the copyrights hereon may be reproduced or used in any form or by any means — graphic, electronic or mechanical, including photocopying, recording, taping or information storage and retrieval systems — without the prior written permission of the publisher.

ACKNOWLEDGEMENTS

Many people have given very generous help and support during the preparation of this book.

We wish to acknowledge the special contribution made by The Christmas Heirloom Company and would like to thank them for allowing us to share their particular vision and the magic they associate so successfully with Christmas.

We thank Peter O'Hagen (Highwic House) and John Webster (Ewelme Cottage) for their patience and help. Special thanks also to our families and friends who coped cheerfully with having their homes being invaded for photography; with treasured possessions disappearing for props — all in the true spirit of Christmas.

CONTENTS

FOREWORD

Christmas is the most sentimental season of the year, a time dedicated to celebrating the birth of Jesus Christ nearly 2000 years ago in the (then) little town of Bethlehem.

The Christmas festival, over the years, has come to embrace values other than those related purely to Jesus. Today, Christmas is a season of peace and goodwill to all, of families, friendship and feasting throughout the world.

In the pages of this unique and beautiful book, you will find much more than the detailed history of the Christmas traditions we celebrate in the 20th century. Inspired by a desire to recapture the true spirit of Christmas, we hope, in so doing, to share with you the magic and romance of the rituals carried out at this hallowed time of the year: the traditional decking of the halls with holly and garlands, the decorating of the tree — the focal point in the family home, the giving of wonderfully wrapped gifts to those we love, and the preparation of sumptuous Christmas fare to be eaten with a sense of occasion.

All of these traditional rites bring a never-ending pleasure into our lives at Christmas, a time which is like no other in the year. We hope you share our vision spread before you on the following pages and that you, have a very Merry Christmas!

SECTION
I

AN INTRODUCTION TO CHRISTMAS

All over the world, children leave a supper for Santa as a reward for climbing down the chimney and leaving their stockings filled with toys — slices of Christmas cake and a glass of port for Santa, and a carrot and an apple for the reindeer.

A nativity scene with hand-painted figures includes the baby Jesus, Joseph, Mary, the Three Wise Men, the shepherd, an angel, plus camels, donkeys and lambs.

A Festive Air

Just before midnight, on December 24, there is an expectant hush all over the world. The night sky is sprinkled with tiny, magical stars. There is a stillness in the air. Small children snuggle down in their cosy beds, daring only to whisper as they listen intently for the jingle, jingle of the bells on Santa's reindeer coming toward their home. Will Santa's sack be large enough for all the gifts they've prayed for over the past few weeks?

In the living room, their parents curl the last ribbon around a gift, attach a tag and sit back on their heels, sighing with relief that they have finished wrapping everything.

For it is Christmas Day on December 25; the day when Christians celebrate the birth of Jesus Christ. The reason for establishing the 25th as Christmas Day is difficult to state with certainty, but it is generally understood that this day was chosen by the Christians to correspond to pagan festivals that took place around the time of the winter solstice — December 22. (The original calendar set January 6 as the date for celebrations, but in 1752 the calendar changed and the date was brought forward eleven days to December 25. It is confusing, but then so much about early Christmas celebrations is!) The date was not set in what was considered the West until around the fourth century, and in the East, not until nearly a hundred years after that.

Not all churches celebrate the birth of Christ on December 25. Armenians follow the old Eastern custom of honouring His birthday on January 6, the day of Epiphany. In the West, this date commemorates the visit of the Magi (the Three Wise Men) to the infant, and in the East, it commemorates Christ's baptism. To modern Westerners, January 6 is also Twelfth Night, when all decorations must be taken down; it is unlucky not to have done so by this date. Yet in Sweden, January 13 is considered the end of Christmas. This day is known as St Knut's Day because Canute (Knut) the Great forbade people to fast in the period between Christmas and the Octave of Epiphany.

The word Christmas derives from the Old English 'Christes Masses' (Christ's Mass) and the way we spell it now came into being in around the 16th century.

Winter solstice was the perfect time to choose to celebrate Christ's birth, for the pagan peoples were already celebrating the rebirth of the sun and the lengthening of the days. In Northern Europe, tribes held a festival of Yule to commemorate the sun as giver of light and warmth. The Roman people, on the other hand, celebrated with the festival of Saturnalia; Saturn was the god of agriculture, and of course the rebirth of the sun was extremely important to the successful growth of crops. A cheerful season of celebrating the spirit of Saturn meant good fortune for the coming year. Saturnalia began on December 17 with religious rites and lasted for seven days; in early Roman times, the festival was marked by much drinking and great feasting and gambling.

Except for the cooks and bakers (who were necessary for the feasting episodes) Romans were not allowed to work during this time. The generally accepted rules of social behaviour were turned upside-down — slaves became free men for the seven days, and from amongst them was chosen a king; the colourful paper hat we find in the cracker has its origins in the tradition of this pagan crowning. The spirit of goodwill to all men and women prevailed during this period. Decorations appeared in houses, and friends and family gave each other small presents as tokens of appreciation.

So it appears that the Christmas period which we still celebrate in the 20th century has its roots in these traditional pagan festivals.

Certainly, the tradition of feasting has remained with us, although the succulent wild boar's head, which used to sit in the middle of a groaning table, has been replaced by a turkey and a leg of ham.

In pagan times, the evergreen tree was revered, signifying a continuing life-cycle; this tree had survived the harshness of winter, and therefore the people could also survive.

Fire was an important element. It symbolised warmth, and some believed that fire kept away the Devil. The yule-log was carried into the home amidst singing and dancing and was lit with a brand from the previous year's log.

Straw and corn also played a vital role in pagan fertility celebrations. Decorations made of corn were hung on the front door and around the house to encourage the good influence of the corn spirit on the forthcoming harvest. For the Christians, straw was a reminder of the humble stable and the manger wherein the Christ child lay.

Some religious scholars hold that the birth of Jesus Christ, hailed as the 'light of the world', was drawn as a parallel to the rebirth of the sun, hence making Christianity more meaningful to the pagans the Christians hoped to convert.

Until the end of the 13th century, the celebration of Christmas was almost entirely based around the pagan festivals. It was St. Francis and the Franciscan monks who led the movement to bring its spiritual meaning to the masses. St. Francis chose the nativity as the most important event in the story of Christ's life and, in 1223, he built a life-size replica of the Holy Family, complete with stable, manger, ox and ass, at the Church of Greccio in Italy. Since that time, the nativity has been re-enacted in churches every year, developing from a religious ritual into the mystery or miracle plays dramatising the coming of Christ.

Christmas became a religious and family celebration, spreading throughout Europe and Great Britain.

However, in 1642, when the Puritans came to power in Great Britain, Oliver Cromwell banned the celebration of Christmas and forced the population to work on Christmas Day. He threatened punishment to those who disobeyed, and Christmas retreated to the home, surviving more in remote country areas where the hand of Cromwell was least powerful.

It wasn't until the reign of Queen Victoria that Christmas was 'rediscovered' as a celebration. There was a sentimental feeling in society at the time, a sense of charity and goodwill and a longing for the great and golden years past. Christmas embodied that humane spirit.

A simple bundle of wheat sheaves is reminiscent of early pagan decorations.

German and English in origin, these Victorian Christmas cards are beautifully detailed with embossing, cut-out shapes and fold-out sections created by sophisticated printing techniques.

Queen Victoria and her consort, Prince Albert, are credited with having introduced the first Christmas tree to the English. The first Christmas card was also produced at this time. John Calcott Horsley, a member of the Royal Academy, designed a card in 1843 in response to a suggestion by his friend, Henry Cole; they had the card printed in 1846, and sold a thousand copies at a shilling each.

The themes of Victorian Christmas cards are virtually all floral. Forget-me-nots feature widely, as do roses. Victorians chose the symbolism of flowers to enhance their Christmas message. Many cards were blank inside and a single-sided postcard form was very popular.

The Christmas card is now a multi-million dollar business, with cards printed in many shapes, sizes and styles. Father Christmas, robin redbreast, snow-covered landscapes, carollers, decorated trees, nativity scenes and stars in a clear blue sky all personify Christmas throughout the world. Modern cards often feature a simple star, or the word 'Peace'. Antipodeans are often sent cards depicting wintery scenes when they are experiencing a heat wave . . . while their European friends laugh when they receive scenes of Santa on the beach under a sun umbrella. Christmas has a humorous aspect to it still.

This unusual New Year card, dated 1876, folds out to become a fan featuring calendar panels and a silk tassel. The profile of Queen Victoria is on the front, along with the date.

The origins of the Christmas carol are mixed. In pagan times, groups of people used to wander from house to house with an empty wassail bowl, hoping to be offered a drink of mulled beer brimming with apples. 'Wassail' derives from the Anglo-Saxon 'wes hol' meaning 'be whole'. Christians consider another Franciscan monk, Jacapone Da Todi, to be the father of the modern Christmas carol, because he encouraged the singing of simple songs in praise of Christ's birth, rather than pompous Latin hymns.

The Victorians embraced carolling fervently. It was a family activity and was also seen by the affluent as a means of dispensing charity. Small groups of singers went gaily from house to house, singing in praise of 'Good King Wenceslas', or 'The Holly and the Ivy', to be paid by the houseowner with either a small coin, a gift of fruit and nuts, or sweets. In 1843, British author Charles Dickens was so moved by the spectacle that he wrote *A Christmas Carol,* a story that has become a classic.

Hand-drawn Christmas polka music rests on a Victorian burr walnut piano, in readiness for a musical evening.

'But Once a Year' is the title of this lithograph, based on a picture by W.L. Thomas, showing Victorian children spellbound by the Christmas pantomime. From The Graphic *Christmas number, 1884.*

It was the Victorians who invented parlour games like charades and blind-man's buff, generally played late afternoon on Christmas Day. It was the one time of the year when all the family gathered together to enjoy themselves — the older members of the family occasionally preferring to snooze.

This was the era, too, of the pantomime, a particularly British tradition whose origins might be traced back to ancient Saturnalian rites. The pantomime is a fairytale performance for the whole family, with extravagant scenery and characters; traditionally it stars a young actress in the male leading role, with men as the comical and elderly female characters. It has become a great theatrical Christmas tradition — a little bawdy in modern times — but the spirit has remained.

This lithographic front cover of Paris Illustré, *dated 1 January 1886, shows the tragedy of the poor child flower-seller as she watches a wealthy child leaving a toy shop, absorbed by her beautiful new doll. This cover is typical of Victorian sentimentality with its moral message — the poor child can only dream of such a doll.*

'Christmas in Canada — A Juvenile Skating Ball' shows the elaborate splendour of such an event. Not only is it a scene of magnificent costumes and massed garlanding, but there is an orchestra to provide the appropriate ball music. From The Graphic *Christmas number, 1883.*

This old toffee tin is brimming with well-loved Christmas ornaments.

Victorian Britain was in the grip of an industrial awakening, and entrepreneurs were quick to see Christmas as a commercial opportunity. As the celebration of Christmas spread, the mass-produced glittering bauble soon replaced the humble candle as a tree decoration, and colourful paper chains hung from corner to corner in the front parlour, instead of the natural evergreen branches.

Mistletoe, named the 'golden bough' by the ancient Druids, had always been credited with mysterious healing powers — it could be used as a remedy against poisons, to induce fertility in men and animals and to scare away the evil spirits. The Victorians hung mistletoe in the hallway and began a ritual we employ today: anyone standing under the mistletoe can kiss whoever walks by (in Victorian times it was the perfect opportunity for young men to snatch a kiss from the young lady they admired).

A Victorian, Mr Tom Smith, is without doubt the man who invented the Christmas cracker. A confectioner's apprentice who turned his hand to making wedding cake decorations, Tom Smith visited Paris, France, in 1847 to look for innovations in the confectionery business that he could take back to Britain. In a small shop window, he saw a display of sugared almonds wrapped in twists of coloured tissue paper; thus the 'bon-bon' was brought to Britain. The public responded well, but demand for the sweets stopped after Christmas. Tom Smith decided to play on the seasonal aspect, by placing messages of endearment inside the wrappers, but he felt there was still something missing. Fortunately, while he was sitting at home listening to the crackle of his log fire, he realised the answer to his problem: he would put a bang into his bon-bons. It took him a further two years of experiments before he invented the saltpetre friction strip. The Christmas cracker was an immense success and manufacturers put just about everything into the cardboard cracker tube.

Today, the cracker is mass-produced and generally contains a rhyme, a paper hat and a small plastic or metal gift. The more expensive the box of crackers, the better the gift — although these days the bang is often a whimper. Modern machines do not take as much care as Tom Smith's workers did in Victorian times. But despite the odd disappointment with what's inside the paper tube, no dinner table would be complete without the cracker, and it's a tradition that's here to stay.

Santa Claus, the jolly fellow clad in red, with his long, snow-white beard trailing almost down to his waist, is another traditional character destined to remain part of the Christmas folklore forever. His origins can be traced back to St. Nicholas, a rather solemn-looking fourth-century Christian Bishop of Myra, and the patron saint of children. He was a charitable soul with a reputation for his good works.

St. Nicholas's Day is December 5, and the first of the season's gift-giving days, especially in European countries like Holland and Belgium. Children were in awe of St. Nicholas, because throughout the year their parents reminded them that although good children would be rewarded, bad children would be punished on December 5.

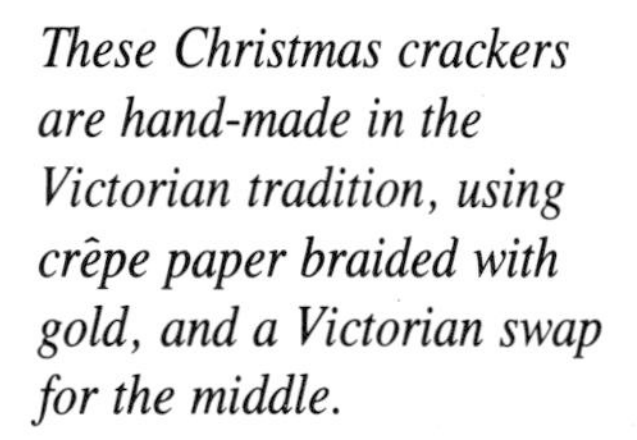

These Christmas crackers are hand-made in the Victorian tradition, using crêpe paper braided with gold, and a Victorian swap for the middle.

In 1822 the American Clement Moore wrote his poem, *'Twas the Night Before Christmas*, about a visit from St. Nicholas.

Yet it wasn't until 1863 that the friendly, ho! ho! ho! character we all know and love came to life in a drawing done by American illustrator and cartoonist Thomas Nast. His first Santa was a small, rotund, elf-ish character dressed in a fur-trimmed red suit and a hat trimmed with sprigs of holly, and carrying a sack bulging with presents.

Santa Claus's reindeer were a later addition. In 1939 an American company, Montgomery Ward, published a children's short story by Robert L. May as a Christmas give-away. It was the tale of a forlorn

LEFT: An early image of Santa Claus on a Christmas card.

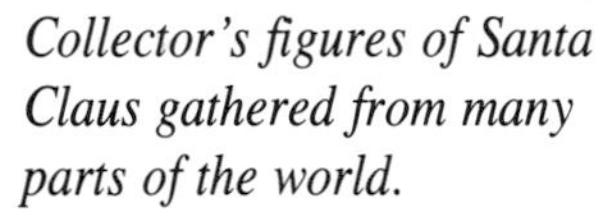
Collector's figures of Santa Claus gathered from many parts of the world.

These Santa Claus figures illustrate the development of the well-known and beloved character who has become synonymous with the celebration of Christmas.

An early image of Santa Claus shows mischievous children taking advantage of Santa's fatigue.

but unexpectedly heroic reindeer in Santa's team. The story was an instant success, with two and a half million copies being distributed in the first year. Rudolph the Red-nosed Reindeer was born and he was to have more than his 15 minutes of fame: he led Dancer, Dasher, Prancer, Comet, Cupid, Donner and Blitzen into Christmas history.

The Americans adopted their celebration of Christmas from the first European settlers who arrived in Virginia in the year 1607. The Germans brought the tree, lit with candles; the Scandinavians, the tradition of a wreath made of fir or pine boughs hanging on the front door as a sign of welcome to family and friends, and of good luck for the coming spring season; the Dutch brought to Manhattan Island the stockings filled with treats in the tradition of St. Nicholas; and Spanish settlers who came to the area now known as Texas contributed their annual ritual of the re-enactment of the journey made by Joseph and Mary into Bethlehem. This celebration, Las Posadas, is a mixture of procession and street theatre, always followed by noisy festivities, at the height of which a pinata, a large and colourful container, is hung from a roof beam. Children strike at this with sticks until it breaks, letting loose an avalanche of presents. These two traditions have survived as an integral part of many Hispanic communities' Christmas celebrations held today.

Americans have the German families to thank for the introduction of exquisite tree decorations. Early illustrations show candle-lit trees decked out with cheerful paper roses, stars and snowflakes made of lead and glass, gilded nuts and apples, cookies, candies, and a wax angel on top.

By 1890 the enterprising Woolworth family were importing German decorations for sale in their stores and the business of Christmas began.

The Americans also imported their carols — from England came 'Good King Wenceslas'; from France, 'Holy Night'; and from Germany, 'O Christmas Tree' and 'Silent Night'. One of the world's most loved Christmas songs, 'Jingle Bells', was composed by an American, Southerner James Pierpont, and, although 'Away In A Manger' has been historically attributed to Martin Luther, the Americans claim it was created in a small Pennsylvania Church.

It was in the 1850s that the first Christmas cards reached America. German-born printer Louis Prang printed his first card designs in the year 1875, popularising floral, religious and Santa themes. But when cheaper cards from Europe came onto the US market in the 1890s, Mr Prang retired from the Christmas card business.

Today's Christmas seal has its origins in America. In 1907, Emily Bissell of Delaware was looking for a way to raise money for a small tuberculosis sanitorium under threat of closure. Emily learnt of a special stamp issued in Denmark to raise money for needy children, so she designed her own, showing a holly wreath and the words 'Merry Christmas'. The seals were sold in a packet with the words:

Put this stamp with message bright
On every Christmas letter.
Help the tuberculosis fight
And make the New Year better.

In Victorian England, seal designs featured flowers, rosy-cheeked young girls, ruddy-faced Santas, train engines, soldiers and many other familiar objects. Used to seal cards and presents, the originals are now collector's items.

Mass-production of modern designs in all sorts of shapes and colours has ensured the seal will remain a popular tradition, while post offices in nearly every country also design and print special stamps to commemorate Christmas.

Most of the rituals we observe in the 1990s have their beginnings in the past. Some have been adapted to suit the particular needs of the country: Antipodeans have resorted to taking the Christmas Day meal outside, either in the form of a barbecue, or a picnic at the beach. Those that insist on true British tradition eat turkey and plum pudding later, in the cool of the evening.

The most remarkable aspect of Christmas is that no matter which country you are in, the hand of friendship reaches out to everyone. It is a time when whole families — sometimes ranging from great-grandmother down to the youngest babe in arms — come together to celebrate. Most do it for religious reasons; others just for the pleasure of the season. Stand at an airport in the days preceding Christmas and watch the homecomings: the rapturous hugs for Mum and Dad and the joy on their children's faces at being home.

Christmas is the one time of the year that can bring people together, a time when all can proclaim 'Joy To The World'.

'The Arrival — Home for the Holidays' is a lithograph from The Graphic *Christmas number, 1883. An elder brother is bid a fond welcome home by his adoring siblings, upon his return from school.*

Entitled 'A Child's Christmas Memories', the banner at the top proclaims Peace on Earth and Good Will towards Men. The series of vignettes portrayed include 'The Sweet Story of Old', 'Stirring the Pudding', 'Hark! The Bells', 'Looking out for the Coach', and 'Snowballing': published in The Graphic *Christmas number, 1883.*

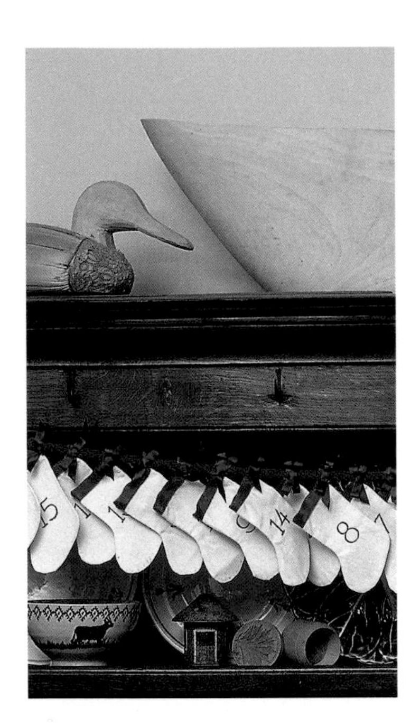

An Advent stocking is another form of an Advent calendar. Children in the family take turn about to slip their hands inside the stocking to see what treat awaits them.

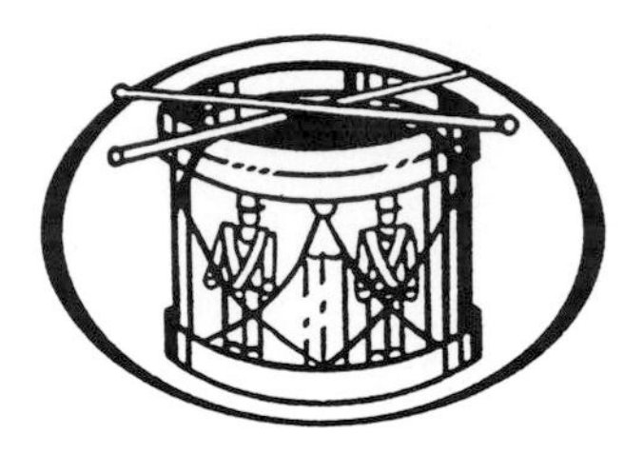

Other Christmas Traditions

The tradition of Advent has its origins in religious ceremonies. The four weeks of Advent (prior to Christmas) symbolise the four comings of the Son of God: in the flesh, in the hearts of believers through the Holy Spirit, at the death of every man, and at the Day of Judgement. The last week is never-ending, for the glory of Christ's coming will never end.

Advent is a period of preparation for Christ's coming, starting on the Sunday closest to November 30, St. Andrew's Day. The season is marked by a series of church services and devotions and, in modern times, by a series of social events, the office party probably stemming from this very tradition. Advent calendars are hung and on December 1, the first door is carefully opened to reveal a Christmas scene, or a delicious chocolate. (It is a sad fact that the chocolate behind the door is more enticing than a Christmas scene to young children these days.) On the same day, the top section of the 24 sections of the Advent candle is lit, as is the first of the four candles on the evergreen Advent wreath.

It is in this period that many theatre groups present the Nativity play, a celebration of Mary and Joseph's trek and the birth of the young Christ-child.

Advent is also the time to make practical preparations for Christmas. Traditionally, houses were cleaned thoroughly; in the country, barns and other outhouses were whitewashed and brought to order.

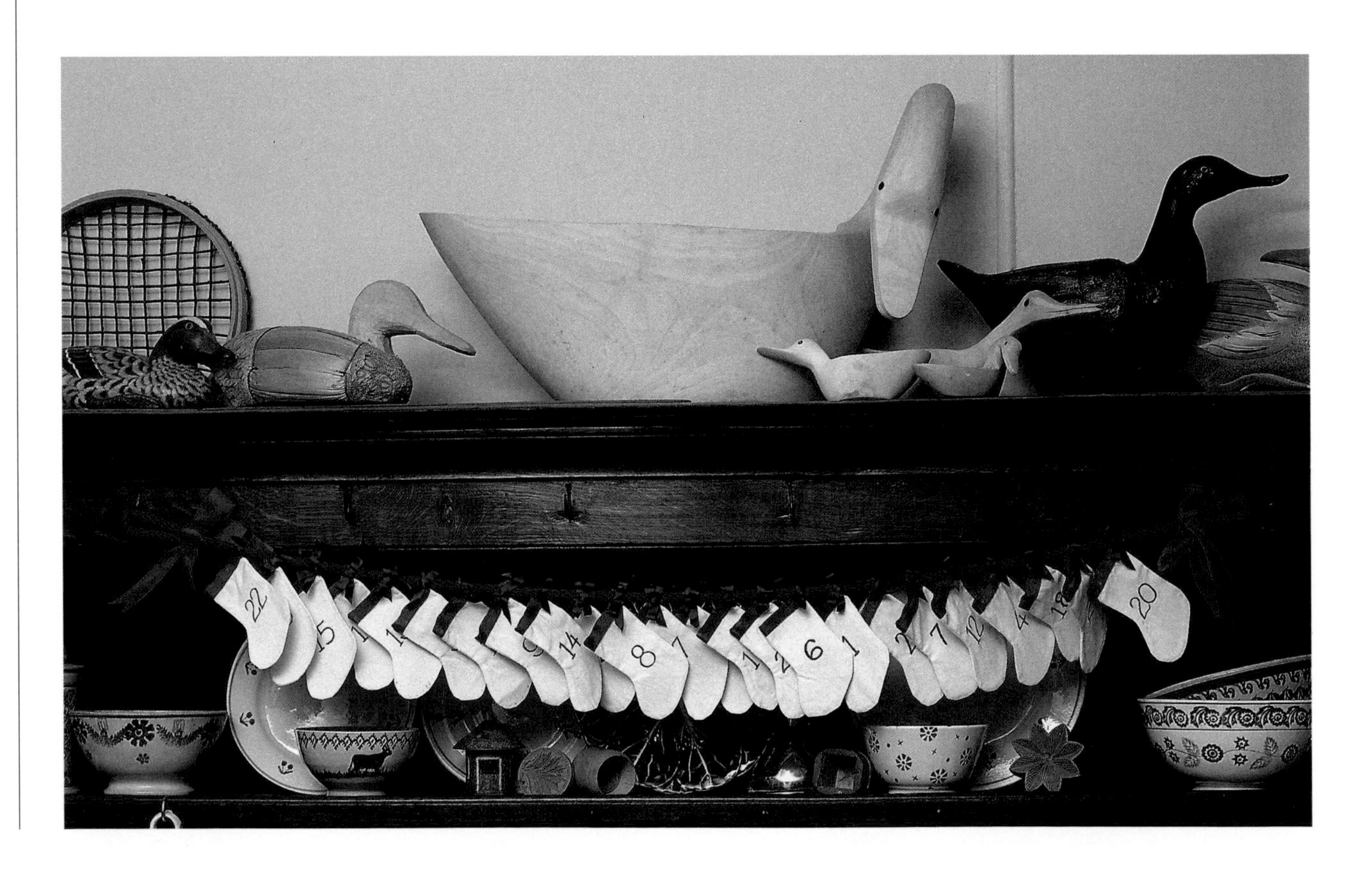

OPPOSITE: A sturdy willow basket encircled by Oregon pine and larch cones, filled with moss and simple white candles, fits well on a Welsh dresser, surrounded by kitchen implements.

LEMON

One of the many stories associated with Robin Redbreast tells of Joseph leaving Mary and the baby Jesus to collect more fuel for the fire. He was absent so long that Mary grew anxious that the fire would go out. Suddenly, some small brown birds appeared, and fanned the fire with their wings. In doing so, they scorched their breasts. Hence the red breast colouring of the robin.

Today, nothing has changed! People send cards and gifts in a flurry of activity just before closing dates, hold small parties with family and friends and prepare the house for the return of sons and daughters and their families. The kitchen becomes the work-centre as food is prepared and stored ready for the Day. The tree is unpacked or chopped down, decorations unpacked, tree lights checked, nativity cribs and figurines put in place and wreaths placed on the front door as a welcome sign. By Christmas Eve, everyone is in a state of excitement and joy at the thought of Christmas.

The day after Christmas has two rituals attributed to it. The first concerns the killing of the wren on St. Stephen's Day. This was the only day upon which the sacred wren was allowed to be hunted; after its death, the wren was paraded door to door around the village, held high on a decorated branch. At some time in history, the robin became mistaken for the wren and that's why the robin redbreast has such a close association with Christmas.

December 26 is also known as Boxing Day when, in Victorian times, the servants downstairs broke open their box of tips.

In Sweden, St. Lucia celebrations begin on December 13, when the daughter of the house, clad in a white robe and wearing a crown of candles, creeps into her parents' bedroom to quietly wake them with a prepared breakfast. Originally, Lucia Day was marked by processions in Swedish towns and villages and it was only in the 1800s that this domestic ritual developed.

Why St. Lucia, a young Sicilian girl martyred in 304 AD for her Christian beliefs, is so closely associated with Sweden is unclear, but legend has it that during a great famine Lucia provided the country with food, her head circled in light. (A more likely explanation could be that her name day, on the old calendar, fell on the shortest day of the year, which was celebrated using candles and fire-lit torches to drive away winter.)

The Swedish custom spread to North America with the immigrants, and Lucia Day is still practised there today. In Sicily, her birthplace, the Eve of Lucia Day was marked by a procession. Men and children with lighted bundles of straw ran through the villages to the piazza, where they threw their torches onto a bonfire. Behind the men was a statue of St. Lucia carrying a tray on which were her eyes; legend has it that she tore them out because they were so beautiful that they tempted a prince to seduce her away from a convent.

Other countries have developed rituals around St. Lucia, but not many have any relevance to her life and it is mainly for the crown of lighted candles and their association with the new light of spring, that Lucia is remembered at Christmas.

LOCAL ADAPTIONS

In countries where Christmas is in high summer, local flowering plants have taken on the significance attributed to the evergreen. In Australia, the *Ceratopetalum gummiferum* is known as the Christmas bush, named by early colonial settlers who wanted to have a Christmas tree of their own even though the temperature there was 30°C. In New Zealand, the red-flowered pohutukawa tree has the same role. The Maoris have a saying that if the pohutukawa flowers before Christmas, it will be a long, hot summer; if it doesn't, then prepare for a sultry, wet Christmas season.

The Americans named a startling red plant, whose flowers are said to resemble the Star of Bethlehem, poinsettia after Dr Poinsett, the man who introduced it to the United States. Now, for many people, the poinsettia has become synonymous with evergreens.

D0486815

A splendid Georgian burnished steel urn provides the perfect base for a large formal floral decoration featuring glorious red poinsettias and tulips, green Helleborus corsicus *flowers, red Pyracantha berries, red tamarillo fruits, and red Leucadendron. Bare branches of birch and larch, the veined leaves of* Arum italicum, *and green holly and ivy foliage, plus long spikes of Heliconia and Japanese anemone seeds, complete the Christmas feeling in this living room.*

DECORATING IN SEASON

Random the golden retriever has a bright red bow as decoration on his collar for Christmas Day.

DECK THE HALLS

Christmas is a wonderful time of year for those who love interior decoration.

A magical transformation comes over the home. In the living room, the visitor is greeted with a profusion of bright green and red foliage bursting out above the doorways, over the mantelpiece, on window sills and the dining table. The traditional fir tree stands shining like a sentinel in the corner of the room. The mood is cheerful; there is an excitement in the air.

The tradition of decorating the house with evergreens can be traced back to Roman times. During Saturnalia, homes were decked out with green branches and holly, and candles were lit to hail the coming of light deep in the middle of a dark winter.

Meanwhile, in pre-Christian Northern Europe, tribes had worshipped evergreens with much more vigour. They saw the evergreen tree as a symbol of the continuation of life through the harshest hours. Mid-winter solstice, celebrated on December 22, the shortest day of the year in the Northern Hemisphere, was a time for feasting and celebration, to commemorate the rebirth of the sun as the giver of warmth and light.

There are some customs which have survived, to be celebrated in a similar way 2000 years later. The yule-log, adapted for the centre of the dining table and set with candles, is one of them, its origins set in the rituals of rural communities. The superstitions associated with the burning of the yule-log have faded as the world has become industrialised and people have moved into cities — try to find an apartment with a fireplace in a zone where you are not allowed to light fires!

A large mirror provides an opportunity to create an effective Christmas decoration. Golden papier mâché angels nestle among holly leaves and bunches of gold berries, preserved beech leaves, and red holly berries. The same theme extends to the mantelpiece, where it is punctuated by a gold bow at each end.

The origins of the word 'yule' are debatable but it seems most likely that it comes from the Norse word 'jol' meaning a heathen feast lasting for 12 days. Hence yule-tide, a celebration associated with feasting and fertility rites. Somehow, the ritual turned into one also honouring the dead spirits, believed to haunt the living at winter solstice. Huge oak logs were burnt in honour of the god Thor; eventually, the burning of the log came to symbolise survival and warmth.

Over the centuries, the tradition spread to Britain. There, the log was brought inside the house amid much singing and dancing, and lit with a brand saved from the previous year's fire. The log was to burn for the whole 12 days — if the log went out by itself, it was a sign of bad luck.

Those who live in the country and are lucky enough to have a large fireplace are able to keep this ritual alive. City dwellers blessed with a fireplace can enjoy a smaller-scale roaring fire to welcome family and friends in the middle of a Northern winter. For those in mild climates at Christmas, the decorated

Roasted chestnuts on the fire are always an enticement to good cheer on Christmas day.

yule-log retains its significance, even though it has been cut down to size.

Evergreens also represented survival. While other trees were bare and brown, the fir tree stood intact. The holly and the ivy, flowering even in the worst of winters, took on mysterious qualities, as did the mistletoe bush. At mid-winter solstice, branches were cut and brought indoors to encourage the sun to come again.

The elegant form of an Italian stone greyhound is garlanded by a simple twist of ivy wreath, surrounded by a bed of lichen and Helleborus corsicus.

These evergreens have a long association with the traditions of Christmas, and prior to that were very much a part of pagan rituals.

CHERRY LAUREL

This plant has been credited with the ability to protect and purify.

BAY LAUREL

This herb was said to represent the spirit of good cheer symbolised by the Christmas festivities.

HOLLY

The Christian church incorporated holly as part of its symbolism. It caused its sharp leaves to become associated with the crown of thorns that Jesus wore on the cross and the red berries to represent drops of His blood.

YEW

This evergreen though poisonous to man is reputed to ward off the evil powers of witches.

THE CHRISTMAS ROSE

The white Christmas rose, known to botanists as the black hellebore because of its black roots, was another popular decoration until the mid-19th century. It was the first of the winter flowers to push through a December soil, and growers used to supply the rose in bulk.

ROSEMARY

Rosemary, with its purple flower and delicate fragrance, was a popular decoration until the mid-19th century. Rosemary was for remembrance, and was also used to decorate the boar's head upon the table.

MISTLETOE

Mistletoe is a curious plant, known for its qualities as a cure — and once as a killer. Ancient Druids refer to it as the 'golden bough', using it as a cure-all, yet according to myth mistletoe was the wood used to make the dart which Loki threw to kill Balder, son of Odin. He was returned to life, but the mistletoe was made to promise it would never bring about harm again.

Mistletoe was said to induce fertility in men, protect against lightning and banish evil spirits. The early Church, in an attempt to attach a religious significance to mistletoe, declared that the Cross was made of mistletoe wood and the tree had shrunk from shame. Today, mistletoe has a romantic connotation for the British.

IVY

Ivy has pagan associations with Bacchus, the god of revelry and is thought to protect against drunkenness.

Christmas is the ideal time for stairs in a hallway to come alive, with a continuous garland of evergreens and berries. Artificial conifer garlands, entwined with Idesia berries, holly, ivy and Japanese cedar branches, are wound through these timber banisters.

A detail showing the rich, lush layers of green and red, and the twists of birch twigs which disguise the florist's wire used to attach them to the stair rail.

ABOVE: A pressed tin trumpeting angel adorns the top of the side garlands, which continue the theme of evergreens, fruit and berries.

This door lintel decoration is Victorian-inspired. A mixed mass of evergreens — conifer and ivy — plus areas of rich colour provided by oranges, apples and artificial bunches of red and yellow berries, with the central motif provided by a pineapple, combine to create a sensational decorative touch above an entrance.

The central decoration of any formal Victorian dining table was likely to be a silver epergne. Here is a formal arrangement of tuberoses, Queen Anne's lace, lilies, maidenhair fern and ivy. A lush hunting green velvet bow with gold fabric trim is tied at the base. Silver side dishes are filled with oranges, plums, and pears.

ABOVE: A country wreath of twisted grape vines clustered with cones, dried holly leaves, moss, and conifer. Its loose form is threaded with scarlet moiré ribbon.

A variety of grey and soft green mosses and lichens are entwined with a gold ribbon, and decorated with larch cones and tiny white feather doves to create a welcome wreath.

THE WREATH

The Christmas wreath, traditionally made of an evergreen branch, is thought to have originated from Christ's crown of thorns; however this could be another myth that grew as the Church tried to

A magnificent door wreath of preserved conifer, pine and larch cones with a central group of artificial Helleborus niger *(Christmas rose).*

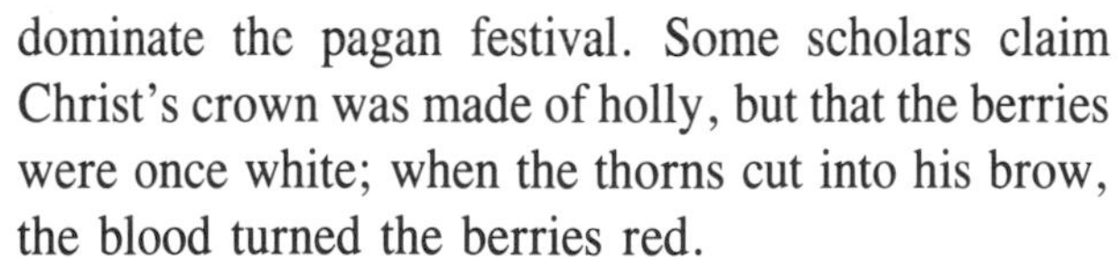

dominate the pagan festival. Some scholars claim Christ's crown was made of holly, but that the berries were once white; when the thorns cut into his brow, the blood turned the berries red.

A wreath for the kitchen, composed entirely of fresh scarlet capsicums entwined with soft green lichen — an unusual but effective decoration for this season.

An entrance hall decoration features a pair of pyramid-shaped baby cone trees flanking a large wooden bowl. The bowl is lined with straw and filled with gourds and fresh persimmon fruit. The central wreath has a straw base with maize, wheat, garlic, chillies, Chinese lanterns, walnuts, cinnamon quills, hazelnuts, artificial peanuts, and tiny pumpkins.

A detail of a glorious mantel garland (more of this over the page) shows trails of ivy, conifer, preserved beech leaves, dried red roses, black reindeer moss, larch and pine cones, dusted with gold so that they glow in the firelight.

OPPOSITE: This clove-studded orange sits on a moss-trimmed stem, formed by upright cinnamon quills. The edge of the terracotta moss-filled pot is broken by fresh lemon leaves. An arrangement like this fits well into a country kitchen scheme.

The full garland shows a swagged effect, which is in keeping with the classic details of this fireplace. An artificial conifer base has been used and fresh conifer added; the sophisticated tartan ribbon tones beautifully with the colours of the dried red roses.

European tribes used to hang a circle of evergreen on their doors as a welcome to friends and strangers, the circle representing a continual cycle of life. Centuries later, European families made Advent wreaths, a circle of a fir branch suspended from the ceiling, decorated with small candles, which are lit one by one on each of the four Sundays before Christmas. This Advent decoration was taken to America by early settlers and is still a popular decoration, although it is not always hung from the ceiling. The fir branch often has small pine cones, dried flowers and herbs woven among the candles.

Many craft-people prefer to make their own door and window wreaths instead of buying a ready-made imitation or plastic one. In recent years, it has been the fashion trend to make wreaths of willow branches, devoid of leaves, but decorated in a country style. To make an Advent wreath, just add the candles and place on a sideboard, entrance hall or dining table.

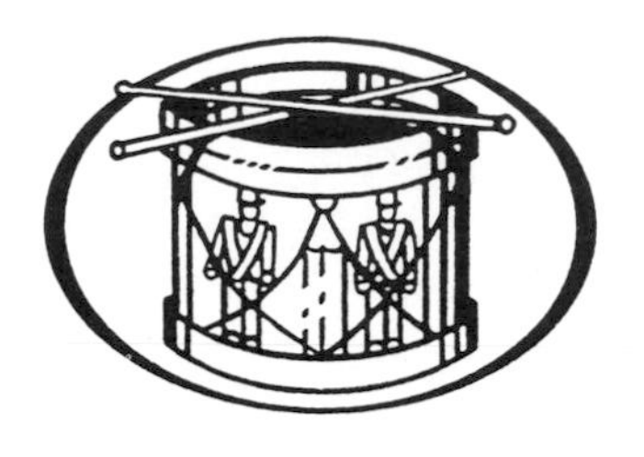

CONTEMPORARY DECORATIONS

These days, true Christmas aficionados leave no surface undecorated. With the commercialisation of Christmas and consequent mass-production of decorations, the decorator's choice is spell-binding. Throughout the world the avid Christmas shopper will discover stores devoted to decorations. For those who do not have access to the real thing, lengths of imitation, evergreen garlanding, with or without berries, look so like the real thing you have to look carefully to notice the difference. When they're wound around staircase banisters, draped across the top of old-fashioned mantelpieces, over doorways and across dressers, the garlanding creates a spectacular effect in any room. Decorated with red and gold berries, baubles or pine cones, such garlanding evokes the original celebratory spirit.

Many families collect nativity figurines, setting these in a place of honour in the room. Mass-produced nativity scenes, with Joseph, Mary and the Baby Jesus, moulded together with the animals and the Three Wise Men, are adequate to portray this religious theme; but the sets with individual figures, hand-carved in wood or clay and painstakingly painted, are preferable as they last a lifetime and can be handed down from generation to generation as an heirloom. Finding straw for the floor of the crib can be a problem, but do not be defeated. You may be able to obain it from an importer, as some manufacturers still ship china packed in straw.

A garland of conifer, beech leaves, clusters of yellow Pyracantha berries, birch twigs, Fatsia berries, purple privet berries, dried Idesia berries, Oregon pine cones, variegated holly leaves, raffia swirls, and an abandoned bird's nest.

A Christmas kitchen theme features a base of artificial conifer entwined with glossy fresh holly and ivy leaves, decorated with garlic, chillies, walnuts and cinnamon quills tied into a bunch with red and gold ribbon, and wish-bones.

A dramatic garland made entirely in the theme of green and gold. Created from an artificial conifer base, it is decorated with birch twigs, gold-tipped larch and pine cones, sprayed gold holly leaves, tiny gold bells, and pierced gold baubles.

A strong red, white, and green theme has been created with bunches of red artificial cherries, tiny tied parcels, and delicate white feather doves. The artificial conifer base is entwined with a scarlet grosgrain ribbon and sprigged with fresh conifer branches.

A mass of dried and preserved flowers forms the basis of this superb garland. Comprised of dried lavender, larkspur, rose-buds, cornflowers, Achillea, larch cones, hydrangea flowers, lichen, Nandina leaves, and birch twigs with bows that repeat the colour spectrum explored in this piece.

A very strong evergreen theme dominates in this garland with masses of dark, glossy leaves, and Fatsia berries, larch cones, variegated holly leaves, dried chillies, and holly berries spread among them.

A hand-made Shaker basket, filled with red Cotoneaster and purple privet berries.

A worn terracotta garden pot, cleverly arranged with black reindeer moss studded with larch cones, makes a stunning mantel arrangement.

Try the effect of an indoor tree made from a lichen ball encircled with twisted birch twigs, and topped with a classic white dove. The trunk is formed by three white birch branches nestled in a lichen-filled worn garden pot.

Here is a terrific idea for a Christmas tree with a contemporary feel. A fine wire grid pyramid, sprayed dark green, is the base for bunches of Idesia berries fastened on with simple silver bows.

A grouping of several terracotta pots will create a stunning effect on a mantelpiece. These contain baby box hedge trees of varying heights; the central topiary tree is made from an artificial base and covered with fresh box leaves. Moss covers the soil in the top of the pots.

A Christmas tableau of nativity figures made of softly draped paper embodies the true spirit of Christmas in a modern manner.

Christmas is the time when small decorative touches can bring a special mood to a room. This arrangement, of soft, creamy, hint of pink miniature roses, privet berries, acmena berries, ivy, maidenhair fern, and magnolia twigs, surrounds the base of a single candle in a pewter candlestick and looks wonderful whether on the dining table or on a hall console.

Resting in an antique terracotta urn, this stunning epicurean pyramid is created from a riot of fresh fruits and vegetables — capsicums, grapes, Callicarpa and privet berries, courgettes and larch cones, Cotoneaster berries, yams, Brussels sprouts, cinnamon quills tied with raffia, moss, box and ivy leaves, mandarins, limes, and Leucadendron flowers.

A willow basket filled with a mass of soft hellebores and foliage is an example of an unstructured arrangement that can come straight from the garden.

A pewter jug filled with purple Anemone *flowers, guavas,* Fatsia *berries, French lavender, privet berries, rosemary,* Ageratum*, box leaves, and acmena berries.*

Candles are an essential decoration for the Christmas festival. Table surfaces covered with a mass of candles cast a magical light.

Set in an antique French cache-pot, surrounded by reindeer moss, a topiary ball shape of dried box leaves, cones, artificial apples, and nuts is a unique table decoration for the Christmas season.

A group of old cotton bobbins is the inspiration for this candle decoration. The central piece is an altar candle set in a small bamboo leaf wreath decorated with lichen, dried Idesia berries, alder cones, and preserved beech leaves. Baby terracotta pots filled with black reindeer moss and white candles, and trimmed with black paper bows, complete the setting.

Old wooden figures of saints are surrounded by beeswax candles in very decorative candlesticks made of alabaster, terracotta, lacquered wood, and wrought iron.

A basket filled with mixed nuts and decorated with raffia-tied cinnamon quills and ribbon-tied cigars, makes a wonderful gift.

A moss basket wreathed in ivy is filled with mixed cones, nuts, and pomander balls.

An inspired red, green, and white table decoration featuring anemones, holly, and nandina leaves, Fatsia berries, ivy, and Arum italicum *leaves is a splendid example of how colour and form can create a festive mood.*

OPPOSITE: A Christmas potpourri scattered in an old gold miner's pan is composed of pomander balls, maize cobs, mixed cones, cinnamon quills, preserved conifer sprigs, beech-nut cases, walnuts, moss, and dried red rose heads. Fragrant and visually pleasing, it can be put in any special place in the house.

Sitting at the end of an antique pine bed — a collection of Christmas stockings. The one on the left bulging with toys is quilted in a Christmas theme fabric. The other two are of the modern knitted variety, incorporating delightful Christmas themes.

THE STOCKING

Children love the Christmas stocking. Whether it hangs on the bedpost or from the mantelpiece, the stocking has an element of wonder for the child. Its origins hail from Holland, where children left out a pair of shoes or clogs filled with hay, water and carrots for St. Nicholas's white horse. They are placed in front of the fireplace, and the next morning the clogs are filled with sweets and small gifts — or the birch rod if the child has misbehaved. Modern stockings are either knitted, made of felt or a quilted fabric. They are always colourful, and are occasion-

ally trimmed with lace or appliquéd. St. Nicholas is now called Santa Claus, but the tradition of filling the stocking with sweets or chocolates (or both) and small, cheap gifts continues. The modern child might find in it a book, a skipping rope, a toy soldier, a sailing ship replica or a pop gun. The fun is in pulling the present out and ripping off the wrapping to find out what Santa did bring.

These hand-stitched stockings made by Lorraine Johnson for her family are a labour of love. Worked in the sampler tradition, they illustrate scenes from the Nativity, and also include appropriate quotations from the psalms.

GIFT WRAPPING

WRAPPING THE GIFT

Most of the pleasure of Christmas lies in the giving, and in the wrapping. There is an art to disguising what's inside the gift paper/bag/box: the more mysterious the package, the higher the level of excitement, particularly for children.

As modern printing techniques have improved and become less costly, so the choice of paper with which to wrap gifts has enlarged. Anything from clear and coloured cellophane and faux-marbleised paper to multicoloured, metallic papers can be found in the best stationers.

Ribbon manufacturers are now responding to the upsurge of interest in gift wrapping and are producing beautiful ribbons and imitation ribbons in varying widths, printed with delightful traditional Christmas scenes and symbols. Velvet, moire and grosgrain fabrics in red, green, shimmery gold and silver are currently in demand, with tartan a perennial favourite. To complete the packaging, decorate it with a small sprig of holly, tiny pine cones, a miniature brass musical instrument or bells.

Gift bags in varying shapes and sizes, printed on heavier weight, glossy papers and usually with a matching gift tag, are a new trend. They are particularly suitable for wine or spirit bottles; other than tie a bow around its neck, there isn't much you can do to disguise a bottle, so the bag is a welcome innovation.

The humble cardboard box is enjoying a resurgence in popularity. With an awareness of recycling, gift-wrappers are seeking out the pure and simple. But the modern box is more sophisticated, better designed and comes in a wide range of sizes. It has the added advantage of being completely reusable: change the colour of the bow tied around it, and you can use it for someone else next Christmas, or for a birthday gift.

Don't just look for ribbons and trims at stationery stores. Treasures like braids, tiny gold and silver tassels, flat woven fabric braids, netting and plaited cords can be found in haberdashery stores. Incorporate a little extra gift with your parcel — attach a Christmas decoration to a bow, or tiny preserved red rose-buds to the centre of an organdy bow.

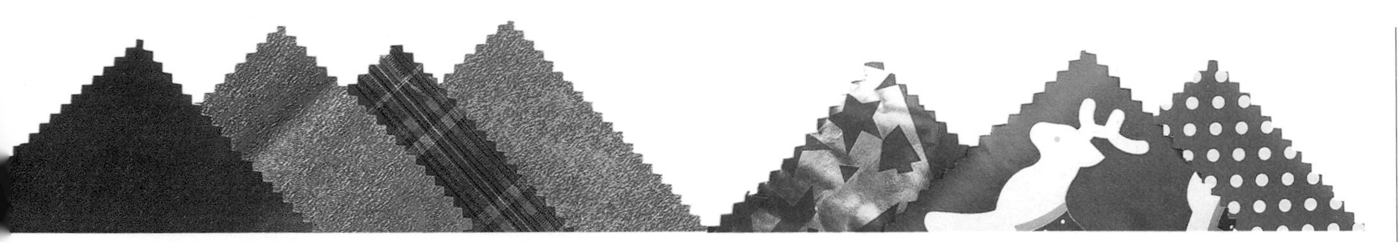

This group has a strong emphasis on gold and white. It is a sumptuous theme for Christmas gifts and there is an enormous variety of finishes available. Foil papers provide the brightest; there are many matt effects available, too. If gold and white is your theme this year, try wrapping gifts in a variety of papers ranging from plain to heavily patterned, and unifying them with a common ribbon.

Bold red, accented with touches of green and white, is this colour theme. Don't be afraid to mix a variety of materials — tissue, dyed wood wool, shiny red cast-coated boxes. Using plain red gloss paper and brightly patterned ribbons and braids is one alternative, and tartan happily mixes with scarlet.

Presenting dramatic effects with combinations of gold and silver, highlighted with an occasional touch of black. If you are packing fragile or awkward-shaped gifts, use a box and fill with a soft packing material that accents your colour scheme, like dyed or printed tissue — get it shredded for volume.

Tones and textures of silver dominate here, with a splash of scarlet added for effect. A variety of ribbons shown includes the double-wired and pleated kind, used on the shirt box in the centre. These are effective for complex bow styles, and they are easily manipulated into interesting shapes.

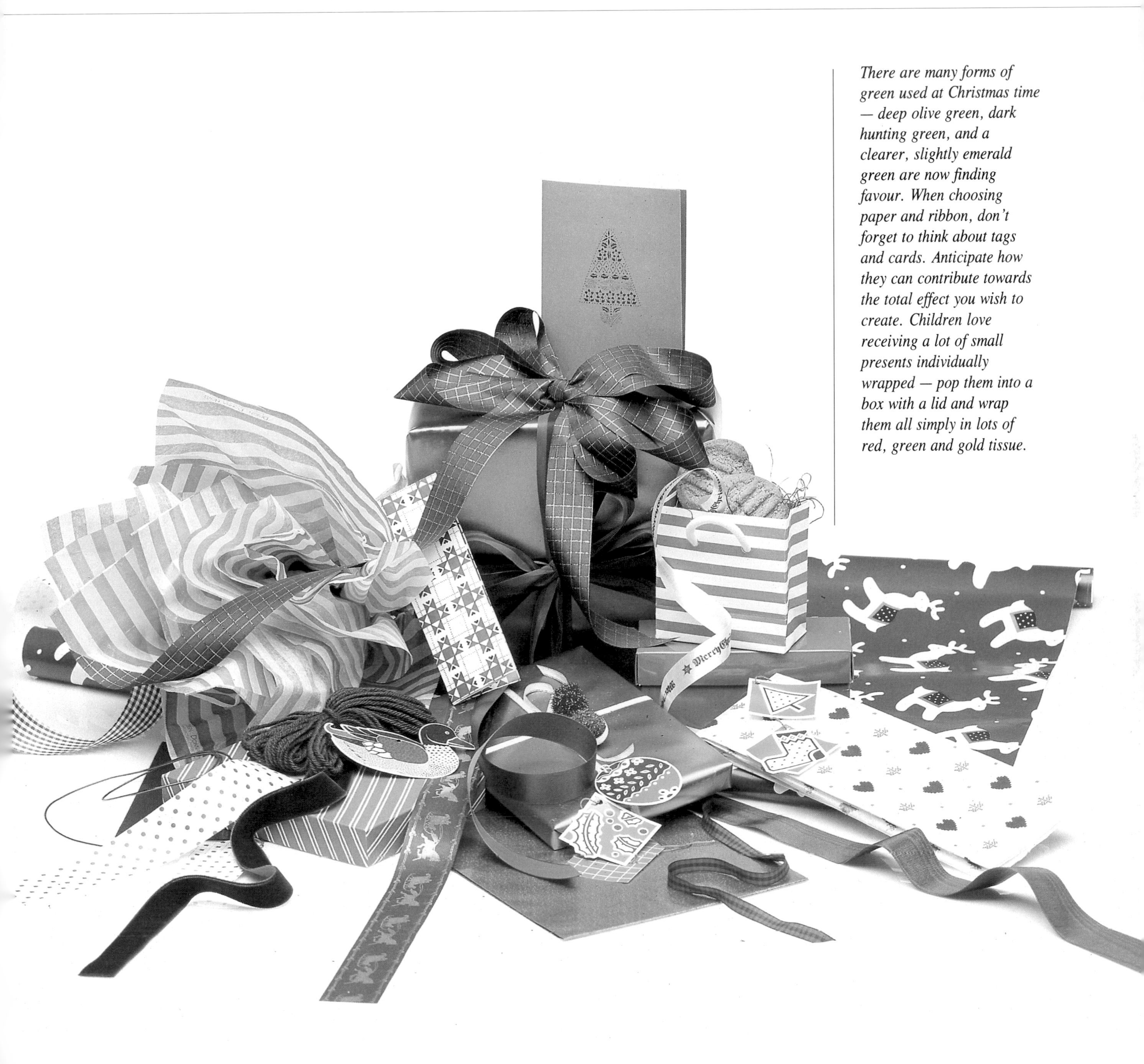

There are many forms of green used at Christmas time — deep olive green, dark hunting green, and a clearer, slightly emerald green are now finding favour. When choosing paper and ribbon, don't forget to think about tags and cards. Anticipate how they can contribute towards the total effect you wish to create. Children love receiving a lot of small presents individually wrapped — pop them into a box with a lid and wrap them all simply in lots of red, green and gold tissue.

Of Angels and Stars

Behold, a gold and white tree festooned with a myriad of decorations — hearts, bells, eggs, and globes beaded with braid and pearls and antique gold-finished fabric bows. Pearl and gold bead wreaths mingle with bright gold apples. The tree is layered with rope beading and fairy lights. Old family teddy bears, dressed for the occasion, wait for Santa.

THE CHRISTMAS TREE

Evergreen and elegant, the tree symbolises an ever-continuing cycle in the pageant of life. The modern celebration of Christmas would not be complete without an evergreen fir tree emanating its majesty and brilliance from a corner of the room.

The evergreen tree was viewed with reverence by Northern pagan tribes for its ability to survive the harshest winter conditions, but it was St. Boniface who can take responsibility for the fir tree now being universally accepted as the Christmas tree. In the eighth century, at the completion of the Christianisation of Germany, he cut down the sacred oak of Odin. Behind it stood a small fir tree, which he immediately dedicated to the baby Jesus.

The Christmas tree custom as we know it was not generally practised until the last century. The man credited with the creation of the tree decorated with candles is Martin Luther who, according to legend, was so enchanted by the sight of a star-lit winter sky through fir-tree branches in the forest, that he went home and attempted to reproduce the sight for his children by placing small, lighted candles on a tree.

The decorated tree did not become accepted in England and Europe until 1841, when Queen Victoria and her consort, Prince Albert, set up a beautifully decorated tree for their children at Windsor Castle. Apples, nuts, fruits, gingerbread, gilt and paper shapes and candles always featured on early trees. The Germans were fond of brightly coloured paper roses, stars, snowflakes made of lead and glass, cookies and candies. A wax angel figure was placed on the top of the tree.

As the art of tree decorating became more popular, craftsmen expanded the range to include tiny trumpets made from twisted straws of glass, hand-blown and painted vases and birds, and fancy globes, which were silvered on the inside or lacquered on the outside. The German candles were works of art, tapered and shaped into spirals to reduce the dripping. Whenever possible, beeswax was used instead of tallow.

Images of a rustic country tree: trails of ivy and holly garlands are punctuated with a variety of red berries, with robin redbreasts and bird's nests, tiny wreaths with small birds, and berries.

Candle-holders, either counter-weighted or spring-clipped, were devised and in later years, special clip-on glass lanterns shaped like flowers or fruits held a small candle and kept the flame away from the tree. Glass-sided lanterns with tiny, oil-burning wicks that floated on water were also hung from branches like ornaments.

When electricity was invented in 1879, the candle became electrified. The first American tree lit up New York City in 1882 with 80 lights of red, white and blue flashing as the tree turned. Domestic versions soon followed and the trend spread to Europe. These days, there are lights in all shapes and sizes from tiny, clear, white bud-lights through to flower or bell-shaped, multicoloured sets that flash intermittently. As we head towards the year 2000, the choice of decorations is fantastic. Christmas is big business throughout the world, with year-round stores devoted to the romance and magic of Christmas.

In the 1970s the silver imitation tree was fashionable, but in recent years the evergreen, living or permanent, has regained the number one position. Various contemporary trends have had their moment of glory, but it is the traditional theme which has proved perennially popular.

A vision of silver and white combines simple elements — foil wired bows, matt finish berries, feather doves and a light dusting of snow.

Toyshop treasures: a delightful mix of tin fire engines, wooden trains and trucks, soldiers, bears, Santas, cats, and geese. A velvet bow and vertically strung beading are elegant finishing touches.

Lengths of gold beading hung with 'tear drops', combined with a myriad of small gold apples, gilded walnuts, stars, lanterns, and finger-sized angels with sweet, painted faces dangling against deep evergreen branches are the basis for a traditional theme. Add fragile, oval and round-shaped, coloured glass balls dipped in glitter, clusters of brass bells with red velvet bows, miniature toy soldiers, painted rocking horses, cherubs, reindeer, merry-faced Santas, small gilt parcels (some with real gifts inside, others just for show) and white bud-lights, to complete the effect.

Traditionally, an angel has reigned on top of the tree, but over the decades the angel has also been portrayed as a fairy, and the Star of Bethlehem has made its appearance, too. Contemporary trees are sometimes seen topped with a large bow made out of lustrous red or green gilt-edged velvet. Wired ribbons make the best kind of bows.

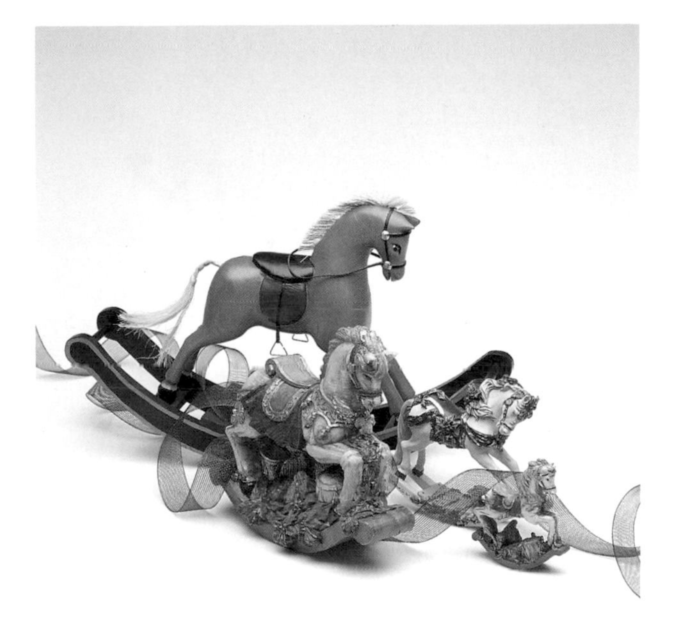

ABOVE: In pride of place, a golden angel trimmed with lace and bows. Her face and hands are hand-painted.
MIDDLE: Christmas fairies and angels watch over festivities.
BELOW LEFT: The Victorian child's rocking horse inspired these heirloom toys.
BELOW RIGHT: Christmas bells are symbolic of the call to worship in the church.

Angels, the messengers of God, have become an integral part of the Christmas story, because an angel was sent to tell Mary of her chosen role in the birth of baby Jesus. These two beautiful angels are made from softly sculpted and painted crêpe paper.

The Tartan 'Hunt Club' tree is decorated with pressed brass hunting horns, tartan papier mâché baubles, velvet, bell-trimmed bows, rocking horses, and tiered brass double-beading. This is a favourite country-style tree.

Tartan and brass decorations, evoking images of a European country lifestyle, are very popular, as are musical, toy and romantic themes. Wooden replicas of alpine houses, cuckoo clocks, birds and animals in painted or natural styles have become collector's items over the years, as have limited editions of Santa Claus, exquisitely moulded and dressed in varying types of finery.

In America, decorations can be ordered with names and phrases engraved upon them. For instance, a small, personalised, brass nameplate with the words 'From our house to your house — with love from the Smith Family' can be ordered in late August for delivery by December. Personalised baubles become family heirlooms hung on the tree each year and as new family members arrive, theirs, too, take a special place amongst the decorations.

The tree is for families. Many like to decorate the tree on Christmas Eve, with members of the family gathered round, making it a memorable experience. Others cannot resist the thrill of decorating the tree weeks before! That way, the presents can pile up underneath it, tantalising everyone who visits. Christmas remains an intensely personal experience for everyone, a time of sharing peace and goodwill among family and friends: the tree and the gifts embody this mood and will continue to do so as long as we celebrate the joy of Christmas.

LEFT: A musical scroll formed by miniature Christmas carols, red and green beading and pressed brass bows, violins and stars.

Fantasy in gold — a tree like this always takes the breath away. Apples, berries, tiny foil and fabric-wrapped parcels, pressed Santa faces, wreaths, parcels, hearts and trees all complete the image. Some of the decorations here are designed to light up when slipped over fairy lights.

ABOVE: A faceted and bead-trimmed Star of Bethlehem shimmers on a tree top. RIGHT: Beading, icicles, mirrored glass baubles, clusters of berries, fabric bows, and a mirrored snow crystal glitter against the green.

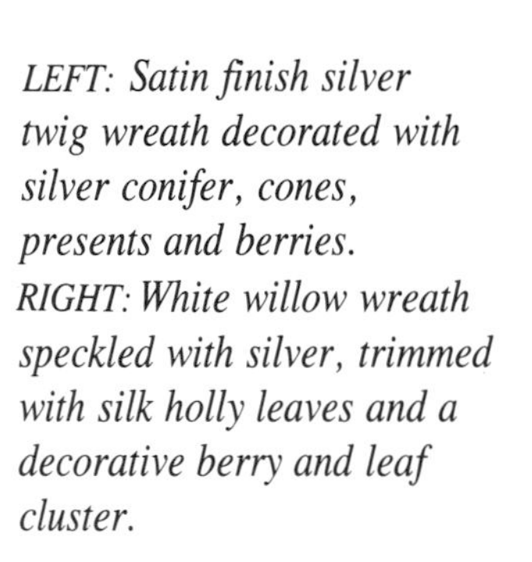

LEFT: Satin finish silver twig wreath decorated with silver conifer, cones, presents and berries.
RIGHT: White willow wreath speckled with silver, trimmed with silk holly leaves and a decorative berry and leaf cluster.

A seaside theme was popular in Victorian times. Triple strings of pearl beading, porcelain sea shells, wooden sailing clippers, pirate's chests and Victorian swaps echo the nautical theme.

LEFT: A delightful clipper in full sail is a delight to a child's eye.
BELOW: Framed plaque of a sailing ship with rope trim is in keeping with the nautical theme.

Two white porcelain angels are lit from inside by fairy lights, creating a soft glow on this tree.

The romance of the Victorian era blooms again in this combination of porcelain, lace, ribbons and bows in pastel shades. Fans, violins, cherubs, porcelain fairies, birds, rocking horses, and delicate organdy ribbon hang together in harmony amidst the evergreen branches.

ABOVE: A tree base is a practical way to secure any tree. Made from cast iron, this design includes a water dish for live trees. MIDDLE: Gold and red lattice design. Lurex ribbons tie into a fabulous tree-topper. TOP RIGHT: A brass scroll of musical notes.

ABOVE: Snow globes, some musical, feature a variety of Christmas themes. RIGHT: A pressed brass horn.

A collection of tree decorations hand-made from pieces of old American patchwork quilts. These add a human touch to any theme tree.

THE FESTIVE TABLE

❖

A Sense Of Occasion

Christmas dinner is without doubt the occasion for an especially impressive table setting. If there was ever a time to use your very best china, linen, crystal, and sterling silver, it is then. Imagine it — the silver shining, glasses gleaming in the candlelight; the table linen crisp and starched, beckoning guests to the table.

A large table is always appropriate for such a grand occasion. It provides that extra space necessary for an unusually large number of glasses, plates, serving dishes, candles and flower arrangements, and space to carve the turkey.

If the surface of your table is of a beautiful wood, or lacquered, simply polish it and allow the glow to show between place-settings — though take care to protect the surface with heat-proof mats. If your table is fairly ordinary, begin the setting by covering it with an interesting cloth . . . rummage through the family linen cupboards to see what's hiding there. White damask, whether well-loved or brilliantly new, looks beautiful with linen or cotton place-mats trimmed with pierced borders, appliqué, embroidery, or lace. Placing a runner of a contrasting colour and texture along the length of the table is effective, especially if you co-ordinate the napkins. The combination of a floor-length cloth layered with a smaller second cloth looks glorious. For extra style, loop table napkins through napkin rings with a Christmas theme, or tie simply with wide tartan bows.

Dinnerware combinations also create different effects upon a table. White or cream china with rich, embossed borders of gold or silver placed on an underplate with an all-over design, or made of pewter, gold or silver, looks superb. Experiment with colour and design, keeping to the rich traditional seasonal shades.

Glasses look best on a formal table if they are fine stemmed and elegant in their design. If you do not have matched sets, try to match the style. Cut-crystal, frosted, etched or gilded glasses suit these special occasions.

Also, be imaginative with serving dishes. Start collecting interesting shapes — maybe find a china goose-shaped soup tureen, a pewter covered vegetable dish; glass-stemmed bon-bon dishes for candied fruits, and perhaps a pair of Victorian celery vases which you could fill with cherries for a delicious effect.

Candles are very important for setting a Christmas mood. Incorporate them into a floral centre-piece, or group them in the centre of the table, near the flowers. Candelabras are good to use because their height allows people to maintain eye contact, and casts a pool of light across the table. Try grouping modern, tall, glass candle-holders to achieve the same effect.

Ensure the highest point of a centre-piece is at the centre of the table and that it descends evenly from this point. Fresh flowers at this time of the year bring a happiness of their own to the table, and they can be cleverly combined with fruit, berries and nuts, as well as with preserved and dried flowers. Masses of flowers of a single colour look terrific, too. Another idea is to place individual posies at each place-setting. Always incorporate a piece of evergreen, especially the gloss of holly and ivy trails.

Christmas crackers are essential, either to match the colour theme or as a contrast. Using place-name cards adds a formal touch to the feast. Use plain cream or white and ask a calligrapher to write the names in gold or silver ink; or, buy a tiny decoration and loop the cord through a hole in the card. Then they can take it home — a keepsake of dinner at your house.

A contemporary look using white German dinnerware with a fluted edge and a partly gilded edge. As an accent, use red tartan place-mats, a tartan runner, and a plain red chintz napkin. Cutlery is modern, with a simple line. A tiny terracotta pot containing a miniature tree made from artificial berries, surrounded by reindeer moss, is tied with black satin ribbon.

Fine English bone china dinnerware with rich bands of gold is complemented by cutlery with a gold and silver finish. The place-mat is of fine white cotton edged with Battenburg lace, and the napkin is linen with a hand-painted gold border. The centre-piece features creamy gold lilies.

Bold Imari-style dinnerware rests on a black moiré taffeta place-mat. The cutlery is a French classic sterling silver design. The 1930s silk chiffon tablecloth is printed with full-blown old roses, with areas worked in gold metal thread. A trio of black lacquer and gold hand-painted eggs in front of a mass of rosehips completes the scene.

This richly decorated dinnerware, though antique, is still manufactured today. It has a transfer base with hand-painting in tones of green and gold on a cream background. The cutlery is very traditional yet simple, with a beaded edge. An old glass with swags, ribbons and gilding sits among fresh conifer and gold artificial holly leaves and berries. The table is swathed in white voile and the starched white damask napkin is tied with a dark green bow.

A sumptuously decorated English plate steals the scene from the side-plate banded in gold. A rich mixture of nuts, cones and leaves sits in a miniature terracotta pot tied with a black paper bow. The table runner is gold gauze with rich Paisley borders.

Crimson and gold combinations feature here. The cutlery is modern with traditional touches and the place-mat, fine white linen with hand-painted drawn thread-work. The centre-piece features preserved red roses.

This exquisite white plate has an embossed border telling the story of The Magic Flute, *the inspiration for this dinnerware. The cutlery has a beaded edge. The cloth is actually a fine antique paisley shawl, and the place-setting is decorated with a bowl of pot-pourri, oil-burning glass candles, and fresh hellebores.*

SECTION II

THE CHRISTMAS FEAST

Food from Cassell's Household Guide *circa 1880.*
TOP LEFT: Open Jelly with whipped cream.
TOP RIGHT: Yorkshire Pie and Aspic Jelly.
CENTRE: Trifle, surrounded by Ices and Jellies.
BOTTOM LEFT: Christmas Pudding.
BOTTOM RIGHT: Jelly of two colours.

FESTIVE FOOD

Ah, the spirit soars at the thought of an ancient British Christmas feast. Several courses of food, accompanied by jugs of ale and followed by sweet pies and cakes are consumed in a convivial atmosphere.

The sacrificial wild boar, slaughtered for the feast, its head taking pride of place on the platter, was the food of kings and noblemen. Alas, the wild boar is no more. He has been replaced by a more tame meal — the turkey and a leg of ham.

The habit of feasting at this time of the year has its origins in the practice of the farming communities who, out of necessity, had to slaughter their stock. The pasture was dead or covered in snow and the beast would have died of starvation. Originally, the slaughter took place in November but from the time of the Roman occupation in Britain, it was moved forward to December.

The pig has traditionally been associated with sacrificial slaughter and, in ancient times, sausages made from a slaughtered pig adorned the head of the wild boar as it was carried into the nobleman's dining room. Later, the peacock became a feast speciality and in Germany and other areas of Europe, the goose was the recognised feasting dish. For many years, the goose was the popular bird for eating, after the extinction of the wild boar.

The turkey, upon which we feast today, was introduced by the Spanish, who brought it back from Mexico in the 16th century.

The Christmas pudding has undergone an interesting transformation from a pie with a meaty middle to one which is sweet and fruity. It was originally made of frumenty, or hulled wheat spiced and boiled in milk; occasionally used as a fasting dish on Christmas Eve, it sometimes accompanied a meat course. Over the years, eggs, dried prunes, and even lumps of meat were added and it was served in a bowl as plum porridge. Gradually, the meat was replaced by fruit mince.

The ritual of stirring the pudding, with every member of the family stirring in the sixpence or the five-cent piece from east to west, in honour of the Three Wise Men, is still a common practice, although the silver coins are sometimes replaced by silver pudding charms. The searching for coins in the pudding is a continuation of the Saturnalian ritual of choosing a leader by drawing lots: whoever found the silver coin was the leader for the period.

Cakes and biscuits always played an important role at festive occasions. In England, the mince pie (once meaty, now of fruit) and the fruity Christmas cake were sufficient at Christmas. It was in Europe that the cakes and biscuits took on various shapes. Oxen and pigs, even the figure of Christ, were made from wheat or oats kept from a previous harvest and baked in the simple hope that the coming year would be good for all.

The Germans, in particular, made delicious, regional, spiced cakes, gingerbreads and marzipans. Spain and Italy have nutty nougats as their specialities, while the French make *pain d'épice* (gingerbread), a cake in the shape of a log called *bûche de Noël,* and doll cakes which they call *naulets.* The Swedish used to bake a loaf in the shape of a wild boar, and the Polish community baked wafers.

Traditional mulled wine is a modern version of the wassail drink — a hot concoction of warmed beer with apples bobbing in its foam. Today's mulled wine contains slices of lemons and oranges, spices, wine and water, but it is offered in the same hospitable manner as it was in ancient times . . . as an affirmation of friendship.

Victorian children delighted in the discovery of a silver charm wrapped in paper inside their slice of Christmas Pudding. These charms all have a meaning — the Bell of Bethrothal, Thimble of Blessedness, Wishbone, Coin of Fortune, Bachelor's Button, and Horseshoe for Luck.

CHRISTMAS CAKES AND PUDDINGS

The Sunday before Advent, or the 25th Sunday after Trinity, is known as 'stir-up Sunday'. According to ancient tradition, it is the day to make Christmas cakes and puddings so they will have time to mature for the Christmas festival.

Classic Christmas Cake

CLASSIC CHRISTMAS CAKE

500 g / 1 lb. sultanas
250 g / 8 oz. raisins
125 g / 4 oz. currants
250 g / 8 oz. mixed peel
¾ cup rum
250 g / 8 oz. butter
2 cups brown sugar, lightly packed
1 teaspoon grated orange rind
1 teaspoon grated lemon rind
4 large eggs
2 cups flour
1½ teaspoons mixed spice
1½ teaspoons cinnamon

Grease and line a deep, 20–23 cm/9 in. cake tin, first with brown paper and then with greaseproof paper; grease the paper lining well. Combine all the fruit and rum in a large bowl. Mix well. Cream the butter and brown sugar together with the lemon and orange rind, and add the eggs. Mix the creamed mixture with the fruits and rum, stirring well. Mix in the dry ingredients thoroughly. Spread the mixture into the prepared cake tin. Smooth the top of the cake with wet hands. Take a sheet of newspaper and fold it lengthwise to 25 mm/1 in. higher than the top of the cake tin. Measure it right around the cake tin, and if one piece won't wrap around it fold another to make up the extra length. Wrap the paper securely around the outside of the cake tin and tie around a piece of string to keep the paper in place; do not use synthetic or plastic string. Place the wrapped cake tin on a baking tray, which has two layers of newspaper folded on top of it; the newspaper must not touch the sides or elements of the oven. Bake at 150 °C (350 °F) for 3–3½ hours. Cake is cooked when a skewer comes out clean.

Southern Comfort Christmas Cake

Feel free to experiment with the liqueur used in this recipe, as you may prefer the taste of Cointreau or Grand Marnier, with their orange-based flavour.

❖

SOUTHERN COMFORT CHRISTMAS CAKE

1 kg / 2 lb. mixed dried fruit
2 tablespoons mixed peel
25 g / 1 oz. glacé cherries
1½ cups Southern Comfort
250 g / 8 oz. butter
250 g / 8 oz. brown sugar
4 large eggs
3 bananas, mashed
375 g / 13 oz. flour
1 teaspoon mixed spice
½ teaspoon baking powder
3 tablespoons orange juice
½ teaspoon vanilla essence
½ teaspoon almond essence

Soak the fruit, peel and cherries overnight in the Southern Comfort. Cream the butter and sugar, add the eggs one at a time, beating well, then the mashed bananas and the fruit soaked in Southern Comfort. Stir in the dry ingredients along with the orange juice, vanilla and almond essences. Bake at 180 °C (350 °F) for 1½–2 hours or until cooked when tested. Allow to cool in the tin.

❖

MARMALADE CHRISTMAS CAKE

125 g / 4 oz. pitted dates, chopped
125 g / 4 oz. dried apricots, chopped
125 g / 4 oz glacé pineapple, chopped
125 g / 4 oz. sultanas
200 g / 6 oz. currants
100 g / 3½ oz. walnuts, roughly chopped
½ cup orange juice
1 cup marmalade
250 g / 8 oz. butter
1 cup brown sugar, lightly packed
4 large eggs
1 cup flour
2 teaspoons baking powder
2 teaspoons ground cinnamon
½ teaspoon ground ginger

Combine the fruit, walnuts, orange juice and marmalade in a large bowl. Cover and allow to stand overnight. Cream the butter and sugar in a small bowl with an electric beater until light and fluffy. Add the eggs, beating well. Stir mixture into fruit, then add dry ingredients. Spread in well lined and greased, deep, 20 cm/8–9 in. cake tin. Bake in a slow oven 150 °C (300 °F) for 2½–3 hours. Allow to cool in the tin.

Marmalade Christmas Cake with Toffee Glaze

TOFFEE GLAZE FOR CHRISTMAS CAKE

Place 250 g/8 oz. sugar and 6 tablespoons water in a saucepan; stir over a gentle heat until the sugar has dissolved. Increase the heat and boil rapidly for approximately 8 minutes without stirring. Remove from the heat and gently stir in 375 g mixed glacé cherries and nuts. Pour immediately over the top of the Christmas cake to decorate. This is absolutely delicious and everyone will love it.

CHERRY AND NUT CHRISTMAS CAKE

250 g / 8 oz. butter
1¼ cups castor sugar
few drops almond essence
5 large eggs
3 cups self-raising flour
½ cup coconut
150 ml / ¼ pint milk
2 cups red glacé cherries, halved
1 cup nuts, almonds, pecans, walnuts, etc. chopped

ICING
4 cups icing sugar
1 teaspoon butter
3 tablespoons hot water
1 tablespoon lemon juice
extra cherries to decorate

Cream the butter and sugar and blend in the almond essence. Add eggs one at a time, beating well. Fold in the flour and coconut alternately with the milk. Mix in the cherries and nuts. Pour into a greased and fully lined 20–23 cm/8–9 in. cake tin. Bake in a moderate oven 180°C (350°F) for 1½–2 hours, or until cooked when tested. Cool.

To make the icing, combine all the ingredients well. Mix to a stiff paste, adding more water if required. Spread over the entire cake and decorate with extra glacé cherries.

This style of Christmas cake is lighter than the more traditional version. It does not need to be made so far in advance, yet will still keep well, and it is delicious with or without icing.

Cherry and Nut Christmas Cake

A traditional, rich Italian cake, this is an ideal cake to post to friends and relatives as it is solid and low in height.

PANAFORTE

200 g / 7 oz. blanched almonds
300 g / 10½ oz. walnuts
½ cup cocoa
50 g / 2 oz. flour
1 teaspoon cinnamon
1 teaspoon mixed spice
½ teaspoon ground nutmeg
300 g / 10½ oz. mixed glacé fruit
100 g / 3½ oz. liquid honey
150 g / 5 oz. sugar
icing sugar for dusting

Toast both almonds and walnuts at 180 °C (350 °F) for approximately 10 minutes. Allow to cool, then chop the nuts coarsely by hand. (The food processor can make nuts oily). Place the nuts in a large bowl with the sifted flour, cocoa and spices: stir to combine. Chop the glacé fruits and add to the bowl. Place the honey in a saucepan and heat gently until runny. Add the sugar and stir well. Increase the heat so that the sugar melts and the mixture comes to a rolling boil; watch carefully that it does not burn. Cook until the mixture reaches the 'softball' stage or 115 °C (240 °F) on a sugar thermometer. Once this stage is reached, pour the mixture immediately into the dry ingredients, mixing quickly with a fork, then, as the mixture cools, knead it with your hands until it is well combined. Press into a greased 20 cm/8 in. round, shallow cake tin and place on an oven tray. Bake for 30–35 minutes at 160 °C (330 °F). Remove from the oven and loosen the sides of the panaforte from the tin. Cool completely and turn out of the tin; serve sprinkled with icing sugar if desired. Cut into thin slivers with a sharp knife. Store for up to 3 weeks in an airtight container.

Panaforte

CHRISTMAS ICE CREAM PUDDING WITH STRAWBERRY COULIS

½ cup raisins
½ cup sultanas
½ cup currants
1 cup red and green glacé cherries
½ cup dried fruit, i.e. apricots, pears, pineapple, etc, chopped
¼ cup brandy
1 litre / 2 pints chocolate ice cream, softened
½ cup blanched almonds, toasted and chopped
½ cup cream

STRAWBERRY COULIS
500 g / 1 lb. strawberries
1 tablespoon sugar
2 tablespoons brandy

Combine the raisins, sultanas, currants, cherries, dried fruit and brandy in a bowl. Allow to stand overnight. Mix together the soaked fruits, ice cream, almonds and cream. Pour into a 5-cup capacity pudding basin. Cover and freeze overnight or until firm.

To serve, immerse the pudding basin in hot water for a few seconds, then cover it with a serving platter, invert and shake gently to remove the basin. Serve with Strawberry Coulis and extra cream.

To prepare the coulis, place the ingredients in a food processor or blender and process until smooth. Transfer to a serving container, cover and refrigerate until required.

PECAN NUT PLUM PUDDING

This pudding has an American flavour, with the addition of pecan nuts. It keeps well.

1¾ cups sultanas
1¾ cups currants
1¾ cups raisins, chopped
250 g / 8 oz. mixed glacé fruits
1 cup pecan nuts, roughly chopped
2 cups flour
pinch salt
½ teaspoon baking powder
½ teaspoon mixed spice
½ teaspoon ground nutmeg
250 g / 8 oz. shredded suet
2 cups brown sugar
250 g / 8 oz. soft white breadcrumbs
1 tablespoon grated lemon rind
6 eggs
150 ml / ¼ pint milk
3 tablespoons brandy

Combine all the fruit with the pecans. Sift the flour, salt, baking powder and spices into a large bowl. Add the fruit and nuts, suet, sugar, breadcrumbs and lemon rind. Beat the eggs with the milk and brandy. Add to the mixture and blend well. Grease one large pudding basin or two medium-sized ones. Pour in the mixture and cover with a layer of greaseproof paper and foil. Tie securely with string. Place in a large saucepan filled with boiling water to two thirds of the way up the sides of the basin. Cover and cook for 6 hours for a large pudding or for 4 hours for two smaller ones; top up with boiling water as necessary. Allow to cool, then replace the covers with fresh paper and foil. Store in the refrigerator. Reheat by boiling a further 2 hours at the time of serving.

Pecan Nut Plum Pudding

CHRISTMAS CAKE PARFAITS

2 cups fruitcake or Christmas pudding, finely chopped
3 tablespoons dark rum
vanilla ice cream
½ cup cream
sliced red and green glacé cherries to garnish

In a bowl toss the fruit cake with rum and leave for 30 minutes. Layer the ice cream and fruit cake in parfait glasses, starting with the ice cream and ending with the fruit cake. Freeze for 30 minutes–2 hours. Whip the cream and pipe it decoratively over the top of each parfait, garnishing with the extra cherries and holly leaves, etc.

SAGO PLUM PUDDING

4 tablespoons sago
¾ cup milk
1 cup soft white breadcrumbs
¾ cup sugar
1 cup mixed fruit
1 tablespoon butter, melted
2 teaspoons mixed spice
30 g / 1 oz. blanched almonds
1 teaspoon baking soda

Rinse the sago and place it in a bowl with the milk, to soak overnight. Next day, combine the sago mixture with the breadcrumbs, sugar, fruit, melted butter, spice and almonds. Stir thoroughly, then add the baking soda, stirring well. Spoon into a greased pudding basin and cover with greaseproof paper, then foil, and tie securely with string. Place the basin in a saucepan filled with boiling water to three quarters of the way up the sides of the pudding basin. Cook for 3 hours, adding more boiling water if necessary.

TRADITIONAL CHRISTMAS PUDDING

375 g / 12 oz. raisins
375 g / 12 oz. sultanas
250 g / 8 oz. currants
185 g / 6 oz. prunes, chopped
1 tablespoon grated lemon rind
100 g / 3 oz. blanched almonds, chopped
1 carrot, grated
250 g / 8 oz. fresh white breadcrumbs
1 cup sugar
1 cup flour
2 teaspoons mixed spice
4 large eggs
¾ cup milk
1 cup brandy
250 g / 8 oz. butter, melted

Grease a 2 litre/8 cup pudding basin. Mix together the sultanas, raisins, mixed peel, currants, prunes, lemon rind, almonds, carrot, breadcrumbs and sugar. Sift the flour and spices, then add to the fruit mixture. Lightly beat the eggs, then add the milk, brandy and melted butter. Stir into the dry ingredients and fruit and mix well. Fill the prepared basin, leaving 25 mm/1 in. space at the top. Cover with greaseproof paper and foil and tie securely with string. Cook in a large pot of boiling water that comes three quarters of the way up the sides of the basin. Replace the lid of the pot and boil gently for 5 hours. Top up with more boiling water as necessary. Remove the basin and allow to cool. On the day of serving, reheat the pudding by boiling in the same manner for 2 hours.

HARD SAUCE

Beat 150 g/5 oz. butter to soften. Gradually beat in 1½ cups of sifted icing sugar. Continue beating until light and fluffy. Stir in ¼ cup brandy and ¼ cup cream. Spoon into the bowl, cover and chill.

Hard Sauce

Traditionally, everyone in the household is encouraged to stir the Christmas pudding or cake mixture, in the belief that, as a result, he or she will receive God's blessing and the wish they make while stirring will come true.

FLAMING THE PUDDING
If you gently warm the brandy in a small saucepan, it will ignite and burn more readily. Remember to place the pudding on a dish with a generous rim, as excess brandy will also ignite and it is best to contain it.

Traditional Christmas Pudding

CREAMY BRANDY SAUCE

Separate 2 eggs. Beat 300 ml/½ pint cream until soft peaks form. Mix in 6 tablespoons brandy. Beat the egg whites until stiff, and gradually beat in ½ cup castor sugar. Continue beating until all sugar has dissolved. Beat in the egg yolks, then fold in the brandy cream.

SNOW FROSTING

1½ cups sugar
2 egg whites
⅓ cup water
½ teaspoon cream of tartar
1 teaspoon vanilla essence

Place all the ingredients except vanilla in the top of a double boiler and beat over the boiling water for 7 minutes, using an electric mixer, until frosting forms firm peaks. Add the vanilla and continue beating until glossy and very thick. Spread over the Christmas cake, using the back of a spoon to make swirls through the frosting. Allow to dry.

ALMOND PASTE

60 g / 2½ oz. icing sugar
60 g / 2½ oz. castor sugar
125 g / 4 oz. ground almonds
½ teaspoon vanilla esssence
½ teaspoon sherry
½ teaspoon lemon juice
¼ teaspoon almond essence
1-2 large eggs

Sieve the sugars into a food processor bowl. Add the almonds and essences. Add one egg and process briefly to combine: if it presses together to form a dough, it is ready; if not, add a small portion of another beaten egg until the mixture forms a dough. Roll out on to a lightly floured surface and press smoothly over the cake.

ROYAL ICING

2 egg whites
500 g / 1 lb. icing sugar
juice of 1 lemon

Beat the egg whites until firm. Beat in the icing sugar, then enough lemon juice to make a soft-textured, thick icing — enough to cover a 20 cm/8 in. cake.

A Chocolate Truffle decorated with Royal Icing and glacé cherries, looks like a miniature Christmas pudding.

Shortbreads, Gingerbreads, Edible Decorations

GINGERBREAD HOUSE

3 cups flour
1 cup wholemeal flour
1 teaspoon baking soda
1½ teaspoons ground ginger
1½ teaspoons ground allspice
250 g / 8 oz. butter, softened
1 cup sugar
1 large egg
½ cup molasses
2 tablespoons lemon juice

Combine the flours, baking soda and spices. Cream the butter and sugar, add the egg, molasses and lemon juice, beating well. Add the dry ingredients to form a stiff dough. Refrigerate for 2 hours. Cut out a pattern to use as a guide for the Gingerbread House. Roll on a lightly floured board and, using the paper pattern as a guide, cut out the sides, front, back and roof sections, etc. of the house. Bake on plain baking trays for 10–12 minutes at 180 °C (350 °F) until dark golden brown. Leave on the tray for 2–3 minutes to firm, then carefully remove to a wire rack to completely cool.

Make up one batch of the recipe for Royal Icing and use as a glue to fix the sides, roof, etc, together. Allow to dry thoroughly for 1–2 hours before proceeding with the second batch of icing to be used to pipe on the decorations, outlines of windows, snow, etc.

This Gingerbread House can be strung with tiny fairy lights, with larger lights inside to create a glow from the windows.

ROYAL ICING

1 egg white
1–2 cups icing sugar
1 tablespoon lemon juice

Beat the egg white with a wooden spoon until frothy. Gradually add enough icing sugar to make a thick icing, then beat in lemon juice thoroughly. Add more icing sugar if needed. The texture should be such that the icing will slip slowly from a spoon when held up but will not actually fall off the spoon.

GINGERBREAD CHRISTMAS COOKIES

3 cups flour
1 cup wholemeal flour
2 teaspoons ground ginger
1 teaspoon mixed spice
½ teaspoon salt
1 teaspoon baking soda
250 g / 8 oz. butter, softened
1 cup sugar
1 large egg
½ cup molasses
2 tablespoons lemon juice

Combine the flours, ginger, mixed spice, baking soda and salt. Cream the butter and sugar until light. Add the egg, molasses and lemon juice, beating well. Add the dry ingredients to make a firm dough. Roll out on a lightly floured surface, and press or cut out the desired shapes, gingerbread people, etc. Bake 10–12 minutes at 190 °C (375 °F). Allow to cool on a wire rack.

Here we have made people, bears, and trees. However, you can make any shape you like: cut out a cardboard template and make Scottie dogs, polar bears, snow crystals or even camels.

Gingerbread Christmas Cookies

TOP LEFT: Christmas Eve Spiced Nut Cake with Caramel Frosting
TOP RIGHT: Panaforte
BOTTOM LEFT: Christmas Fudge and Christmas Candy
BOTTOM RIGHT: Marmalade Glazed Ham

TOP LEFT: Mince Pies and Tarts
TOP RIGHT: Chocolate Peppermint Creams
BOTTOM LEFT: Gingerbread Christmas Cookies
BOTTOM RIGHT: Classic Christmas Cake

1
2
3
4
5
6
7
8
9

SUGAR CRISP COOKIES

2½ cups flour
¼ teaspoon salt
250 g / 8 oz. butter, softened
1 cup sugar
1 large egg
2 teaspoons grated lemon rind
½ teaspoon vanilla essence

Combine the flour and salt in a bowl. Cream the butter and sugar, and beat in the egg, lemon rind and vanilla. Mix in the dry ingredients until combined. Roll into a ball, cover and refrigerate overnight. Preheat the oven to 180°C (350°F). Divide the dough evenly into four pieces. Roll out the dough between two sheets of waxed paper or plastic wrap to 3 mm/⅛ in. thick, and cut into the desired shapes with cookie cutters. Bake 8–10 minutes until the edges are golden; cool on wire racks. Makes 6 dozen cookies.

CHRISTMAS MACAROONS

2⅔ cups flaked coconut
⅔ cup sugar
¼ cup flour
¼ teaspoon salt
4 egg whites
1 teaspoon almond essence
1 cup almonds, finely chopped
red and green glacé cherries for garnishing

Combine the coconut, sugar, flour and salt in a bowl. Stir in the egg whites and the almond essence. Stir in the almonds and mix well. Drop teaspoonfuls of the mixture onto lightly greased baking sheets. Garnish with a red or green glacé cherry. Bake at 150°C (300°F) for 20-25 minutes, or until the edges of the cookies are golden brown. Remove from the baking trays immediately and allow to cool on a wire rack.

TRADITIONAL SHORTBREAD

2 cups plain flour
2 tablespoons rice flour
⅓ cup icing sugar
250 g / 8 oz. butter, cut into pieces

Sift the dry ingredients and add the butter, rubbing in using fingertips. Press the mixture together. Turn onto a lightly floured surface to knead gently. Divide evenly into two. Mould into rounds about 1 cm thick on greased baking trays. Decorate the edges with fingers or a fork. Mark out eight equal portions, then prick well with a fork. Bake in a slow oven 160°C (315°F) for 30–35 minutes. Remove from the oven and allow to stand for 10 minutes before transferring to a wire rack to cool. Store in an airtight container.

Alternatively, cut into finger shapes or press the mixture into shortbread moulds that have been well dusted with cornflour. Flatten the base and turn out onto greased baking trays. Bake as above.

BROWN SUGAR PECAN NUT SHORTBREAD

2 cups flour
1 cup pecan nuts, roughly chopped
250 g / 8 oz. butter, softened
1 cup brown sugar, lightly packed

In a food processor, grind the flour with the pecans. Cream the butter and the brown sugar, and add the pecan flour. Chill the dough for 2–3 hours. Roll out on a lightly floured surface and cut into the desired shapes. Bake on trays lined with baking paper at 150°C (300°F) for 20–25 minutes. Allow to cool on wire racks.

1. *Almond Crescent Cookies*
2. *Christmas Macaroons*
3. *Cinnamon Scroll Cookies*
4. *Traditional Shortbread (pressed)*
5. *Brown Sugar Pecan Nut Shortbread*
6. *Sugar Crisp Cookies*
7. *Meringue Walnut Kisses*
8. *Mini Christmas Cake Cookies*
9. *Traditional Shortbread (round)*

These shortbreads and cookies are ideal Christmas gifts. Set aside a day for baking; once the oven is hot, do several batches as each has a short cooking time.

MINI CHRISTMAS CAKE COOKIES

1½ cups glacé dried fruits, finely chopped
½ cup raisins
½ cup currants
½ cup brandy (or apple juice)
¾ cup brown sugar, firmly packed
80 g / 3 oz. butter
1 large egg
1 cup flour
½ teaspoon baking soda
2 teaspoons mixed spice
1 cup walnuts
glacé cherries and walnuts for garnish
apricot jam for glaze

Marinate the fruits in brandy (or juice) overnight. Cream the butter and sugar, and add the egg. Add the sifted dry ingredients, then stir in the walnuts and marinated fruits. Spoon into mini muffin tins lined with paper baking cups. Fill three-quarters full. Top each with cherries and walnuts. Bake at 150 °C (300 °F) for 20–30 minutes. Remove from the tins, brush the tops with brandy, (or juice), while still warm. Before serving, glaze with melted, sieved apricot jam. Makes 5 dozen.

ALMOND CRESCENT COOKIES

250 g / 8 oz. butter
½ teaspoon almond essence
¾ cup icing sugar
2 cups flour
½ teaspoon salt
1 cup rolled oats
½ cup finely ground almonds
extra icing sugar for dusting

Heat the oven to 190 °C (375 °F). Beat the butter and almond essence until fluffy, then gradually beat in the sugar. Add the dry ingredients and mix well. Add the rolled oats and the almonds. Shape to form crescents. Bake 15–18 minutes until lightly golden. Sift the icing sugar over the crescents, while still warm.

CINNAMON SCROLL COOKIES

2 large egg whites
½ cup sugar
½ cup flour
1 teaspoon cinnamon
50 g / 2 oz. butter, melted

In a small bowl, beat the egg whites until peaks form. Gradually add the sugar, beating until stiff. Stir together the flour and cinnamon. Fold into the egg whites, then add cooled, melted butter. Place 2–3 tablespoons on a greased baking sheet, spreading each out to form a 6 cm/2½ in. circle. Bake only two or three at a time. Bake at 180 °C (350 °F) for 6–7 minutes or until the edges are golden. Immediately roll the cookies around the handle of a wooden spoon or similar, and slide onto a wire rack once the cookie will hold its own shape. If the cookies become too stiff to roll, re-warm them in the oven for one minute. If desired, the ends can be dipped in melted chocolate.

MERINGUE WALNUT KISSES

1 large egg white
½ cup sugar
1 teaspoon vanilla essence
¼ teaspoon salt
1 cup cornflakes
½ cup walnuts

Preheat the oven to 190 °C (375 °F). Beat the egg whites until frothy. Add the sugar a little at a time, beating well after each addition. Beat in the vanilla and salt. Increase the speed of the beater and continue beating until peaks are stiff. Fold in the cornflakes and walnuts. Drop spoonfuls onto greased baking trays. Bake 20–30 minutes until dry to the touch. Allow to cool for 10 minutes on trays, then transfer to wire racks to cook completely. Makes 24.

❖

CHRISTMAS TREE DECORATION COOKIES

250 g / 8 oz. butter, softened
1 cup sugar
3 large eggs, beaten
⅓ cup brandy
1 teaspoon mixed spice
4 cups flour

Cream the butter and sugar, and beat in the eggs, brandy and the mixed spice. Add the flour and work the dough until smooth. Shape into a roll and chill for one hour. Working on a lightly floured surface, roll the dough out to 5 mm/¼ in. thick. Stamp out the desired shapes with cookie cutters, and place the cookies on baking trays. Use a toothpick to make a hole near the top of the cookie for inserting a ribbon through after baking. Bake at 190 °C (375 °F) for 8–10 minutes. Allow to cool on wire racks. Decorate as desired when completely cold, with Royal Icing.

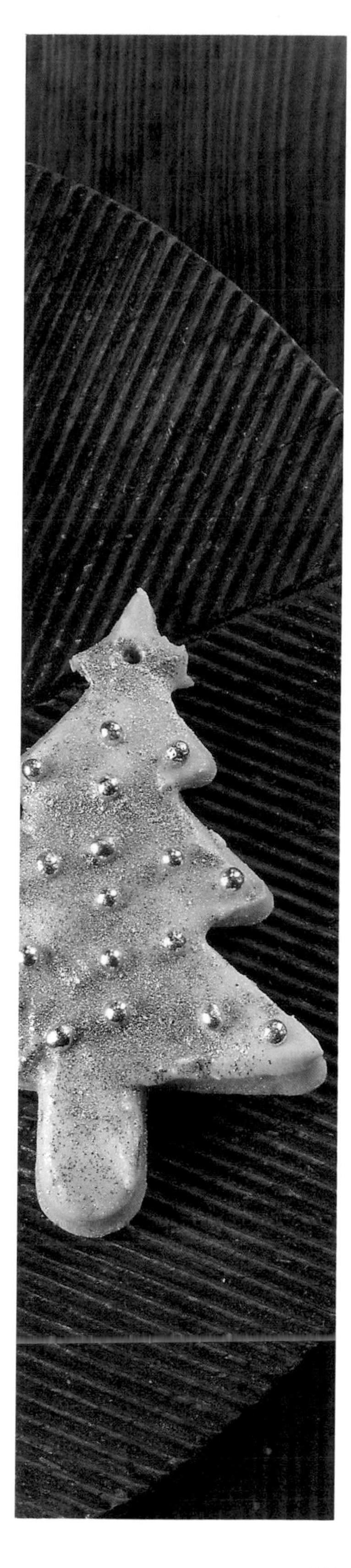

Christmas Tree Decoration Cookies

MINCE PIES AND TARTS

Short Pastry
Traditional Christmas Mincemeat
Macadamia Nut Tarts
Pumpkin Rum and Raisin Tartlets
Cranberry Walnut Tart

Large pie on the left-hand side: Pumpkin Rum and Raisin Pie. The recipe that appears on page 138 is for tartlets, although in our photograph it appears as a large pie. On the footed dish — left-hand side, Cranberry Walnut Tart and individual Christmas Mince Pies; on the right is a Macadamia Nut Tart. On top of the table on the right is a large Christmas Mince Pie. Miniature Mince Pies are in the foreground.

MINCE PIES

SHORT PASTRY
1⅓ cups flour
130 g / 4¼ oz. butter
⅓ cup sugar
1 egg yolk — make up to ¼ cup with ice-cold water

Place the flour, butter and sugar in a food processor and process until crumbly. Add the egg and water, processing in short bursts until the mixture binds together. Do not over-process. Chill for 30 minutes and roll out. Bake at 180 °C (350 °F).

To make miniature mince pies, cut out circles to fit greased mini muffin pans, and the same number of pastry caps. Fill with Traditional

Mincemeat, and place pastry caps on top, pressing slightly around the edges to seal. Bake for 15–20 minutes. Sprinkle with the sifted icing sugar before serving.

To make small mince tarts, press pastry evenly over the base and up the sides of individual tart tins. Fill with Traditional Christmas Mincemeat. Bake for 20 minutes. Serve either with a dollop of whipped cream on each tart, or bake small Christmas shapes and place one on top of each tart.

To make one large mince pie, line a 20–23 cm/8–9 in. pie dish with short pastry and blind bake for 15 minutes. Fill with Traditional Christmas Mincemeat and return to the oven for a further 10–15 minutes. The top may be covered with more pastry, latticed, topped with a Christmas shape pastry cut-out, or whipped cream.

❖

TRADITIONAL CHRISTMAS MINCEMEAT

250 g / 8 oz. grated suet
juice and grated rind of 1 orange
juice and grated rind of 1 lemon
125 g / 4 oz. mixed peel
125 g / 4 oz. blanched almonds, chopped
125 g / 4 oz. glacé cherries, chopped
75 g / 3 oz. dried apricots, chopped
75 g / 3 oz. glacé ginger, chopped
250 g / 8 oz. currants
½ teaspoon salt
½ teaspoon grated nutmeg
½ teaspoon mixed spice
250 g / 8 oz. brown sugar
2 large green cooking apples, peeled, cored and finely diced
500 g / 1 lb sultanas
500 g / 1 lb raisins
1½ cups brandy

Place the suet, orange and lemon rind, mixed peel, blanched almonds, cherries, apricots, ginger, currants, salt, spices, brown sugar, fruit juices, and apples in a large bowl and stir well to combine. Finely chop the raisins and sultanas in a mincer or food processor and place in the basin with the fruit, breaking up any lumps that have stuck together. Stir very well and add the brandy, stir again and leave to stand overnight. Next day, stir well again to blend the fruits thoroughly. Store in clean, sterilised, airtight jars.

MACADAMIA NUT TARTS

1½ cups flour
2 tablespoons sugar
½ teaspoon salt
½ teaspoon cinnamon
½ teaspoon ground ginger
¼ teaspoon ground nutmeg
100 g / 3½ oz. butter
4–5 tablespoons orange juice
1 large egg
½ cup liquid honey
50 g / 2 oz. butter, softened
1 tablespoon flour
½ teaspoon vanilla essence
1 cup macadamia nuts, finely chopped

Combine 1½ cups flour, sugar and spices in a bowl. Rub in the 100 g/3½ oz. butter. Gradually stir in enough orange juice to make a dough. Press two teaspoons of dough into small patty tins, and chill for 30 minutes. Beat the egg until very thick, then gradually beat in the honey, the 50 g/2 oz. butter, flour and vanilla. Stir in the nuts. Spoon into the pastry cases and bake at 180 °C (350 °F) until the tops are bubbly and browned — 12–15 minutes. Allow to cool, and remove from the tins.

In the 17th century, mince pies were large dishes filled with mixed meats, fruits, and spices. Today's Christmas mince is a sweeter fruit and spice filling, with the only remnant of the earlier version being the inclusion of suet.

Both these recipes reveal an American influence and are a lighter alternative to the traditional suet-based based Christmas mincemeat.

PUMPKIN RUM AND RAISIN TARTLETS

PASTRY
1⅓ cups flour
130 g / 4¼ oz. butter
⅓ cup sugar
1 egg yolk — make up to ¼ cup with ice-cold water

FILLING
½ cup raisins
¼ cup dark rum
½ cup sugar
¾ teaspoon ground cinnamon
¼ teaspoon ground nutmeg
¼ teaspoon ground cloves
2 large eggs, beaten
1 cup pumpkin purée
½ cup milk
⅓ cup cream
extra cream to garnish

To make the pastry, place the flour, butter and sugar in a food processor and process until crumbly. Add the egg and water, processing in short bursts until the mixture binds together. Do not over-process. Chill the mixture and roll out onto a lightly floured surface to 1 cm/½ in. thick. Cut into rounds to fit 8 small 10 cm/4 in. tart pans; roll the rolling pin over the tart pans to trim away excess dough.

In a small bowl, let the raisins soak in rum for 1 hour. Drain, reserving the rum. Divide the raisins among the tart shells. Whisk in a bowl the rum, spices, sugar, eggs, pumpkin, milk and ⅓ cup of cream; pour the mixture over the raisins in the tart shells. Bake on a baking tray in the lower part of the oven for 10 minutes at 220 °C (425 °F). Reduce heat to 180 °C (350 °F) and bake another 20–25 minutes, until a knife inserted in the centre of a tart comes out clean. Allow to cool on wire racks for 10 minutes in the tins, then carefully turn out to cool completely. Garnish with piped rosettes of whipped cream if desired.

CRANBERRY WALNUT TART

PASTRY
1⅓ cups flour
2 tablespoons sugar
pinch salt
100 g / 3½ oz. butter, chopped
1 large egg yolk, beaten with 1½ tablespoons iced water

FILLING
3 large eggs
1 cup brown sugar, lightly packed
⅔ cup golden syrup
50 g / 2 oz. butter, melted and cooled
1 teaspoon vanilla essence
1½ cups cranberries
1 cup walnuts, roughly chopped

To make the pastry, place the flour, sugar, salt and butter in a food processor. Blend until the mixture resembles breadcrumbs. Add the yolk and water and process until it binds together. Chill for 1 hour. Roll out to ½ cm thick, to fit a 23–25 cm/10–11 in. tart pan with a removable rim. Chill for 30 minutes. Blind bake the shell for 15–20 minutes at 210 °C (425 °F).

To make the filling, in a bowl whisk together the eggs, brown sugar, golden syrup, butter and vanilla until the mixture is smooth, then stir in the cranberries and walnuts. Pour into the shell and bake at 180 °C (350 °F) for 40–45 minutes or until golden. Allow to cool completely on the rack. Remove the rim of the pan and slide the tart onto a serving plate. Serve with whipped cream.

CHOCOLATE TRUFFLES

125 g / 4 oz. butter
250 g / 8 oz. icing sugar
125 g / 4 oz. dark chocolate or chocolate chips, melted
4 tablespoons cocoa flavouring: either 2–3 tablespoons of your favourite liqueur, e.g. Grand Marnier, Drambuie, or alternatively a few drops of essence, e.g. coconut, peppermint
optional extras: chopped nuts, dried apricots, crystallised peel
Melted dark chocolate to dip truffles in, or chocolate hail, coconut, etc. to coat truffles in

Cream the butter and icing sugar in a food processor or large bowl. Add the melted chocolate, cocoa and flavouring. Stir in any optional extras and chill the mixture for about an hour or until firm enough to roll into little balls. These can be rolled in hail or coconut at this stage, or they can be chilled for a further hour, then dipped into the melted chocolate.

Rich Chocolate Truffles.

Christmas Stollen Bread.

CHRISTMAS STOLLEN BREAD

100 ml / 3 fl.oz. lukewarm milk
10 g / 1½ teaspoons active dried yeast
pinch sugar
25 g / ¾ oz. butter
225 g / 7 oz. flour
¼ teaspoon salt
grated rind of 1 lemon
30 g / 1 oz. blanched almonds, chopped
50 g / 1½ oz. sultanas
50 g / 1½ oz. currants
75 g / 2 oz. mixed peel, chopped
1 large egg, beaten
200 g / 6 oz. almond marzipan
extra icing sugar to dust

Put the warm milk, yeast and a pinch of sugar into a bowl. Stir and leave until frothy, approximately 15 minutes. Rub the butter into the flour and salt and mix in the lemon rind, dried fruit and chopped almonds. Add the yeast mixture with the beaten egg and mix thoroughly until it forms a soft dough. Knead the mixture lightly on a lightly floured surface for approximately 5 minutes, incorporating a little more flour if the dough gets too sticky. Place in an oiled bowl, cover with a clean cloth and leave to double in bulk for approximately one hour. Knead until smooth and shape into an oval. Mark the approximate centre of the oval lengthways and carefully mould the marzipan into a long sausage-shape along the centre mark. Fold one half of the dough on top of the other, completely enclosing the marzipan in the centre. Place on a baking tray, cover with a clean cloth and leave to rise for 40 minutes until doubled in size again. Bake at 200 °C (400 °F) for 30 minutes, until well risen and golden. Remove from the oven and transfer to a wire rack to cool. Dredge thickly with icing sugar and wrap in cellophane.

Home-made gifts are really appreciated by people, not just because they are always far more delicious than the equivalent, mass-produced item, but also because you have taken the time to make them.

Irish Whisky Cream Liqueur

IRISH WHISKY CREAM LIQUEUR

4 cgg yolks
400 g / 14 oz. can sweetened condensed milk
300 ml / 10 fl.oz. cream
3 tablespoons chocolate-flavoured dessert topping
2 teaspoons coconut essence
450 ml / 15 fl.oz. whisky

Beat the egg yolks until thick and creamy. Stir in the condensed milk, cream, chocolate topping, coconut essence and whisky. Mix thoroughly and bottle. Store up to 3 weeks in the refrigerator.

There are many ways to make your home-made goodies look attractive as gifts. Containers are important: look out for little tins, glossy boxes with lids, open baskets, gift bags, and glass containers. Line containers with coloured or printed tissue paper, and use masses of cellophane and beautiful bows.

1. *Minted Apple Jelly*
2. *Miniature Mince Pies (recipe page 136)*
3. *Chocolate Truffles (recipe page 139)*
4. *Christmas Spice Cookies*
5. *Brandy Butter Pecan Loaf*
6. *Fetta Cheese Preserve*
7. *Rosemary Cointreau Spiced Nuts*
8. *Apricots in Brandy*

Bake some special-shaped cookies and include the cutter as part of the gift. A nice touch for your epicurean gift is to include a hand-written card with the recipe.

CHRISTMAS SPICE COOKIES

225 g / 7 oz. butter
225 g / 7 oz. sugar
2 teaspoons golden syrup
1 large egg
350 g / 11 oz. flour
1 teaspoon baking powder
2 teaspoons mixed spice

Cream together the butter and sugar. Slowly drizzle in the golden syrup while the rotary beaters are still going. Add the egg and beat until well blended. Mix in the dry ingredients. Roll into balls or put teaspoonfuls onto a greased baking tray. Flatten slightly with a fork before baking for 15 minutes at 180 °C (350 °F).

FETTA CHEESE PRESERVE

450 g / 15 oz. fetta cheese
100 g / 3 oz. black olives
few sprigs fresh rosemary
1 large onion
450 ml / 15 fl.oz. olive oil

Cut the cheese into 2 cm/¾ in. cubes and place in a preserving jar with the olives. Add the fresh rosemary. Peel the onion and slice into rings, then arrange these over the cheese. Pour over enough olive oil to cover the cheese. Seal the jar and leave it to marinate in the refrigerator for at least one week before serving.

Preserved cheese will keep in the refrigerator for up to 3 months, as you can keep adding fresh cubes of cheese to the marinade to replace eaten ones. By the time you have finished all the cheese, the olive oil will have absorbed the delicate flavours and will make a delicious addition to any dressing.

BRANDY BUTTER PECAN LOAF

125 g / 4 oz. butter
100 g / ¾ cup pecan nuts
4 large eggs
310 g / 12 oz. sugar
150 ml / 5 fl.oz. cream
250 g / 8 oz. flour
2 teaspoons baking powder
pinch salt
75 ml / 3 fl.oz. brandy

Preheat the oven to 160 °C (325 °F). Line the base of a loaf pan with baking paper. Grease thoroughly and lightly dust with flour, carefully shaking out the excess. Melt the butter and add the pecans. Stir over a gentle heat for approximately 5 minutes until the nuts are dark brown. Drain the nuts, reserving the butter. Let the butter cool and coarsely chop the pecans. Beat the eggs, gradually adding the sugar, then the cream and beat thoroughly. Reduce the speed of the beater and mix in sifted dry ingredients until just combined. Add the brandy and pecans, stir, then add ½ cup of the reserved butter, mixing until well combined. Pour into the prepared pan and bake for approximately 1½ hours. Allow to completely cool on a wire rack, then seal in plastic wrap. Leave at least one day before cutting. Freezes well.

MINTED APPLE JELLY

1 kg / 2½ lb. medium-sized cooking apples
1½ litres / 7 cups water
100 ml / 3 oz. lemon juice
⅓ cup fresh mint, chopped
750 g / 1 lb. 8 oz. sugar
2 tablespoons extra chopped mint

Chop the unpeeled apples (being careful not to discard the seeds). Combine the apples, seeds, water, juice and mint in a large saucepan. Bring to the boil, reduce the heat, then simmer covered for 45 minutes. Strain through a fine muslin cloth or jelly sieve into a large bowl. Allow the liquid to slowly drip through the cloth or sieve. Do not squeeze or press the pulp, as this will make for a cloudy jelly. Discard the pulp. Measure the apple liquid, pour into a large clean saucepan and add ¾ cup of sugar to each cup of liquid. (The mixture should be no more than 5 cm/2 in. deep). Stir over a low heat until all the sugar has dissolved, then bring to the boil and boil uncovered for 30 minutes or until the jelly sets when tested on a cold saucer. Remove from the heat and allow to stand for 15 minutes. Stir in the extra chopped mint. Pour into hot, sterilised jars and seal when cold.

ROSEMARY COINTREAU SPICED NUTS

3 tablespoons soya bean oil
2 tablespoons Cointreau liqueur
3 cups mixed nuts: pecans, blanched almonds, macadamias etc.
1½ teaspoons dried rosemary, crumbled
1 teaspoon salt
1 teaspoon mixed spice

In a bowl whisk the oil and Cointreau. Add the nuts, toss and marinate for 15 minutes. Spread the nuts in a shallow baking pan. Toast in a preheated oven 180 °C (350 °F) for 25 minutes or until golden. In a bowl combine the rosemary, salt and spice. Toss the hot nuts in the spice mixture until coated. Lay the nuts out on paper towels to cool completely. Store in an airtight container.

APRICOTS IN BRANDY

To fill a 300 ml/½ pint jar:

approximately 24 plump dried apricots
100 g / 4 oz. sugar
2 cinnamon quills
200 ml / 7 fl oz. brandy (approximately)

In a medium saucepan place the apricots, sugar and cinnamon quills. Barely cover with water and gently poach over low heat for 10 minutes. Drain off the liquid and hold in reserve. Discard the cinnamon quills. Pack the apricots in a sterilised 300 ml/½ pint jar and add half the liquid, then top up with the brandy. Seal the jar and allow to mellow for six to eight weeks before eating.

If you are giving jellies, fruit mincemeat or preserves, make your own labels with decorative borders in red and green, or with other suitable Christmas themes.

Extremely delicious
Chocolate Peppermint Creams.

CHOCOLATE PEPPERMINT CREAMS

60 g / 2½ oz. butter
1 teaspoon vanilla essence
2 level tablespoons icing sugar
¾ cup flour
1 tablespoon cocoa powder
350 g / 12 oz. dark dipping chocolate, melted

MINT CREAM
325 g / 11 oz. icing sugar
1 tablespoon soya bean oil
60 ml / 2 fl.oz. milk
¼ teaspoon peppermint essence

Cream the butter, icing sugar and vanilla essence. Add the sifted flour and cocoa. Mix well. Roll out the dough between two sheets of plastic wrap to a 3 mm thickness. Cut out circles from the dough using an approximately 3 cm/1½ in. plain cutter. Place the biscuits about 2 cm/1 in. apart on greased oven trays. Bake for approximately 8 minutes at 180 °C (350 °F). Stand for 3 minutes and then transfer to a wire rack. Spread the tops of the biscuits with a level teaspoon of warm mint cream, then stand on wire racks until set. Dip the biscuits in the melted dipping chocolate. Stand on greaseproof paper until set.

To make mint cream: In a bowl combine the sifted icing sugar, oil, and enough milk to make a firm paste. Mix in the essence.

CORIANDER CHICKEN SATAYS

500–600 g / 1 lb. chicken breasts, boned and cut into strips approximately 7 cm x 2 cm
5 tablespoons lemon juice
2 tablespoons soya bean oil
6 tablespoons dark soy sauce
freshly ground black pepper and salt to taste
4 cloves garlic, crushed
3 tablespoons fresh coriander / cilantro, chopped

Whisk the marinade ingredients together and add the chicken strips; cover and marinate overnight in the refrigerator. If using bamboo skewers, put them in cold water to soak. Thread the strips lengthwise onto the skewers (push the skewer straight down the centre of the strip). Barbecue over a steady heat or grill quickly, turning to brown all sides. Serve with Ginger Minted Yoghurt Dipping Sauce.

Coriander Chicken Satays

GINGER MINTED YOGHURT DIPPING SAUCE

3 spring onions, finely chopped
200 g carton / 7 oz. plain sweetened yoghurt
3 tablespoons fresh mint, chopped
3 teaspoons fresh ginger, grated
1 clove garlic, crushed
a fresh sprig of mint to garnish

Combine the yoghurt with all the other ingredients, then store in the refrigerator until required. Store covered in the refrigerator for up to three days.

MINI CHEESE MUFFINS WITH SMOKED SALMON AND CAVIARE

2 cups flour
4 teaspoons baking powder
1 large cupful grated tasty cheese
1 egg
¼ cup soya bean oil
1½ cups milk
pinch salt
sour cream
smoked salmon, thinly sliced
caviare
sprigs of dill or parsley to garnish

Mix the top seven ingredients together with enough milk to form a runny, porridge-consistency dough. Don't over-mix as the dough needs to be quite soft, so it is pourable. Spoon the mixture into well greased mini muffin tins. Sprinkle with a few shreds of grated cheese on the top of each muffin, for a glossy finish. Bake in a hot oven 200 °C (400 °F) for 10–12 minutes, until well risen and golden brown. Carefully scoop out a small portion in the top centre of each muffin and fill with sour cream, a small slice of smoked salmon, a tiny dollop of caviare and a sprig of dill or parsley. Makes 24 mini cocktail-size muffins.

OPEN HOUSE COCKTAIL PARTY

Coriander Chicken Satays with Ginger Minted Yoghurt Dipping Sauce
Mini Cheese Muffins with Smoked Salmon and Caviare
Salmon Caviare Toasts
Savoury Blue Cheesecake
Christmas Spicy Nibble Mix
Fresh Fruit Kebabs
Baby Quiche with Lemon Shrimp
Chocolate-Dipped Strawberries
Merry Morsel Pudding Bites
Mini Pecan Pies

Mini Cheese Muffins with Smoked Salmon and Caviare.

Salmon Caviare Toasts.

Savoury Blue Cheesecake.

SALMON CAVIARE TOASTS

10 slices of thick toast-sliced bread
3 tablespoons unsalted butter, softened
125 g / 4 oz. salmon caviare
lemon wedges

Preheat the grill. Cut off the crusts and spread with butter on one side only. Grill until golden brown, buttered side up. Cut each slice into four triangles. Spoon the caviare on the toasted side and serve with lemon wedges to garnish. Makes 40 portions.

SAVOURY BLUE CHEESECAKE

BASE
180 g / 6 oz. butter
500 g / 1 lb. wheaten biscuit crumbs
120 g / 4 oz. ground walnuts

FILLING
50 g / 2 oz. butter
500 g / 1 lb. cream cheese, softened
250 g / 8 oz. blue cheese, crumbled
2 cloves garlic, crushed
4 tablespoons fresh parsley, chopped
2 tablespoons grainy mustard
¼ teaspoon freshly ground black pepper
1 teaspoon Worcestershire sauce
4 large eggs

Heat the oven to 180°C (350°F). Use a tablespoon of the butter to grease two sponge roll tins 30 x 20 cm/12 x 8 in. In a bowl combine the biscuit crumbs and walnuts; add the melted butter and mix well. Press into the base of the sponge roll tins.

In a saucepan, melt the butter over low heat. In another bowl, cream the softened cream cheese, add the melted butter, crumbled blue cheese, garlic, parsley, mustard and pepper until well mixed. Beat in the Worcestershire sauce, then the eggs one at a time. Pour over the base and bake for 30–40 minutes. Turn the temperature off and leave the cheesecake in the oven for a further 15 minutes. Allow to cool and cut into portions. Makes 50–60 bite-size portions.

CHRISTMAS SPICY NIBBLE MIX

1 kg / 2 lb. raw peanuts
250 g / 8 oz. butter
4 tablespoons curry powder
4 packets caramel-flavoured popcorn
2 large packets ready-to-eat crispy noodles
1 cup mixed red and green glacé cherries

Roast the peanuts in the butter and curry powder for 45 minutes at 180°C (350°F) stirring frequently. Stir in the caramel popcorn, noodles and glacé cherries. Mix well. Allow to cool and keep in an airtight container until ready to serve.

Christmas Spicy Nibble Mix

Fresh Fruit Kebabs

BABY QUICHE WITH LEMON SHRIMP

3 sheets ready-rolled puff pastry
1½ cups tiny cooked shrimps
1 cup cream
4 large eggs, lightly beaten
2 teaspoons lemon rind, finely grated
freshly ground black pepper and salt to taste

Cut circles from the pastry, using a fluted, 6 cm/2½ in. cutter. Press into shallow patty pans or mini muffin tins. Divide the shrimps between pastry cases. Combine the cream, eggs, lemon rind, salt and pepper and spoon over the shrimps: the pastry cases should be only two-thirds full. Bake at 200 °C (400 °F) for 10 minutes, or until puffed and golden brown. Makes approximately 36.

Baby Quiche with Lemon Shrimp

FRESH FRUIT KEBABS

500 g / 1 lb. strawberries
6 kiwifruit
1 pawpaw/papaya
1 pineapple or the equivalent in canned pineapple pieces
white-fleshed melon
large black or green grapes
bamboo skewers

Line a tray or plate with bamboo fronds, or ginger-plant leaves. Peel and cut the fruit into bite-sized chunks. Thread a piece of each fruit onto the bamboo skewers; continue until all the fruit is used up. Natural yoghurt mixed with sour cream makes a nice dipping sauce. Garnish the platter with exotic flowers, such as hibiscus, orchids, etc.

CHOCOLATE-DIPPED STRAWBERRIES

1 kg / 2 lb. strawberries, wiped clean
250 g / 8 oz. dark chocolate
250 g / 8 oz white chocolate

Chill the strawberries well. Melt the dark chocolate, then one at a time dip each strawberry into the chocolate to coat. Place on a baking tray which has been covered with greased foil. Continue until all the strawberries have been dipped. For the white chocolate-dipped strawberries, repeat the procedure using the melted white chocolate. Refrigerate until ready to serve.

Chocolate-dipped Strawberries

Merry Morsel Pudding Bites

MERRY MORSEL PUDDING BITES

500 g / 1 lb. moist fruit cake or boiled fruit pudding
a little brandy
royal icing
red and green glacé cherries, chopped

Using a melon baller, scoop out balls of cake. Roll the balls between your hands if necessary, to make them smooth. Brush lightly with the brandy to flavour. Allow to stand a while to dry. Prepare the royal icing and pipe or smooth it over the tops of the balls, allowing it to drizzle slightly over the sides. Sprinkle with the cherries. Allow to stand until firm. Makes 36.

ROYAL ICING

1 egg white
1–1¼ cups icing sugar
a few drops lemon juice

Beat the egg white until frothy, then gradually add the icing sugar, beating constantly until the mixture stands in stiff, glossy peaks. Beat in the lemon juice.

MINI PECAN PIES

125 g / 4 oz. butter
1 cup flour
½ cup icing sugar
1 large egg
1 cup brown sugar
¼ teaspoon vanilla essence
¼ teaspoon salt
60 g /2½ oz. butter, melted
½ cup pecan nuts (or walnuts), chopped

Whizz the butter, flour and icing sugar in a food processor until they cling together. Divide the mixture into 24 pieces and press into the bases and up the sides of well greased, shallow patty pans or mini muffin tins. Beat the egg and brown sugar together, and add the vanilla, salt and melted butter. Mix in the chopped pecans. Spoon the mixture evenly into the prepared pans and bake for 15–20 minutes at 180 °C (350 °F) until the pastry is golden and the filling puffed and crisp. Allow to cool on a wire rack.

Mini Pecan Pies

CHRISTMAS EGGNOG

6 large eggs
¾ cup sugar
1½ cups brandy
½ cup rum
4 cups milk
4 cups cream
½ cup icing sugar
nutmeg to sprinkle

Separate the eggs. Beat the yolks gradually, adding the sugar while beating until they are pale and golden. Slowly beat in the brandy and rum, then beat in the milk and half the cream. Just before serving, whisk the egg whites until stiff and fold them into the eggnog mixture. Whip the remaining cream and icing sugar until thick. Top each glass of eggnog with a dollop of sweetened, whipped cream and a sprinkle of nutmeg.

Christmas Eggnog

CHRISTMAS BEVERAGES

①
②

1. Wassail Cup
2. Sparkling Cranberry Blush
3. Maple Christmas Punch
4. Mulled Wine

When pouring a warm drink into a glass, run the fluid over the back of a teaspoon inside the glass in order to prevent it cracking.

WASSAIL CUP

4.5 litres / 8 pints water
4 cinnamon quills
2 teaspoons whole cloves
8 tea bags
1 cup sugar
150 ml / 5 fl.oz. orange juice concentrate
½ cup lemon juice

In a large saucepan heat the water, cinnamon sticks and the cloves until boiling. Turn off the heat and add the tea bags, orange juice concentrate, lemon juice and sugar. Let them steep for 10 minutes. Remove the tea bags and cinnamon quills and serve.

MAPLE CHRISTMAS PUNCH

2 cups lemon juice
3 cups maple-flavoured syrup
2 cups water
4 cups whisky
ground nutmeg
lemon slices

In a large saucepan, mix the lemon juice and maple-flavoured syrup and water. Heat until just boiling. Stir in the whisky and heat through without boiling. Serve at once in small glasses. Slip a lemon slice in each glass and sprinkle with nutmeg.

SPARKLING CRANBERRY BLUSH

2 cups thawed frozen cranberry juice concentrate
4 bottles chilled sparkling wine, cider or sparkling apple juice
1 cup fresh or thawed cranberries to garnish
mint leaves

Mix the cranberry concentrate and sparkling wine, cider or apple juice in a large punch bowl. Float mint leaves and whole cranberries to garnish. Ladle into punch cups or champagne glasses to serve. Makes 24 servings.

MULLED WINE

4 bottles Burgundy-style red wine
10 whole allspice
6 cinnamon quills, approximately 5 cm/2 in. long
finely peeled rind of an orange
15 whole cloves
½ cup sugar

Combine all the ingredients and gently heat but do not boil. Allow to sit on the heat for 30 minutes, without boiling. Strain into a warm punch bowl and serve in punch cups or glasses.

HEARTY POTATO AND SWEETCORN CHOWDER

4 rashers bacon, finely chopped
30 g / 1½ oz. butter
3 large onions, chopped
2 tablespoons flour
2 cans (440 g / 14½ oz.) creamed sweetcorn
4 cups milk
4 medium-sized potatoes, peeled and diced
2 egg yolks
2 cups cream
2 tablespoons parsley, finely chopped

Cook the bacon in a large saucepan until lightly crisp. Add the butter and onions and sauté until the onions are soft. Add the flour and stir well. Add the potato, sweetcorn and milk, stirring, then bring to the boil. Simmer for approximately 15 minutes until the potatoes are soft. Gradually stir in the combined egg yolks and cream. Season to taste with salt and freshly ground pepper and stir in the parsley just before serving.

CHEESE PUFFS

3 cups grated tasty cheese
2 cups flour
4 teaspoons baking powder
2 large eggs
¾ cup milk

Preheat the oven to 250 °C (500 °F). Mix together the cheese, flour and baking powder. Beat the eggs and milk together, then stir into the dry ingredients. Place teaspoons of the mixture on a greased baking tray and put this in the oven. As soon as you close the oven door, turn the heat right off and cook for 10 minutes on stored heat. Remove and allow to cool on a wire rack.

Hearty Potato and Sweetcorn Chowder and Cheese Puffs.

TREE TRIMMING MENU

Hearty Potato and Sweetcorn Chowder
Cheese Puffs
Spinach, Fetta Cheese and Red Pepper Phyllo Pie
Green Salad
Mocha Truffle Fudge Cake

Layered spinach and red pepper are perfect Christmas colours. This deep-dish pie is easy to prepare in advance and pop into the oven while you spend time with your guests.

SPINACH, FETTA CHEESE AND RED PEPPER PHYLLO PIE

15–20 spinach leaves
1 large onion, finely chopped
250 g / 8 oz. fetta cheese
150 g / 4 oz. Cheddar cheese, grated
1 large red pepper, finely diced
8 sheets packaged phyllo pastry
6 large eggs, well beaten
75 g / 2½ oz. butter, melted

Wash and shake dry the spinach leaves, trim off white stalks and shred finely. Combine the spinach and onion in a large bowl and stand for 1–2 hours. Drain off the excess liquid. Mix in the crumbled fetta and Cheddar cheese with the red pepper. Line a greased baking dish or large pie plate with four sheets of the phyllo pastry, brushing between each layer with melted butter. Spoon the spinach mixture over the pastry and evenly pour in the beaten eggs. Cover with the remaining sheets of phyllo, brushing between each layer with melted butter, then brush the top with melted butter. Bake in a medium oven 180°C (350°F) for 35–40 minutes until the filling has set and the pastry is crisp and golden brown. Serve hot, cut into slices.

Spinach, Fetta Cheese, and Red Pepper Phyllo Pie

MOCHA TRUFFLE FUDGE CAKE

100 g / 3½ oz. dark cooking chocolate
100 g / 3½ oz. butter
1 cup castor sugar
2 large eggs
½ cup flour
¼ cup self-raising flour
½ cup milk

FILLING AND TOPPING
2 teaspoons instant coffee powder
1 tablespoon brandy
300 ml / 11 fl.oz. cream
1 tablespoon castor sugar

Melt the chocolate. Cream the butter and chocolate with sugar and then add eggs one at a time, beating well. Beat in the flours and milk. Pour the mixture into a greased, deep 20 cm/8 in. cake pan, which has the base lined with greaseproof paper. Bake for approximately 1 hour at 150 °C (300 °F). Stand a few minutes before turning out onto a wire rack to cool. Split the cake and fill with the cream mixture. Spread the top and sides of the cake with the remaining mixture and decorate with praline, fresh fruit, strawberries, etc. if desired. To make the filling and topping, dissolve the coffee in the brandy. Add to the cream with the sugar and beat until firm peaks form. Refrigerate the cake for at least 1 hour before serving.

Mocha Truffle Fudge Cake

PRALINE

½ cup mixed nuts, pecan nuts, hazelnuts, walnuts and almonds
½ cup sugar
2 tablespoons water

Combine the sugar and water in a saucepan, stir over low heat until the sugar is dissolved. Boil the mixture rapidly without stirring until it turns golden brown. Stir in the nuts then pour the mixture onto an oiled baking tray. When the praline has set solid, chop up into chunky pieces and sprinkle over the cake.

Praline can be made in advance and stored in an airtight container for all occasions. It is a great standby in emergencies — try it as an ice cream topping, or mix it into softly whipped cream.

Midnight Church or Carol Singing Supper

Spicy Pumpkin Soup
Thyme Croutons
Festive Lasagna
Apple Cake
Eggnogg Ice Cream

❖

SPICY PUMPKIN SOUP

100 g / 3½ oz. butter
1 cup finely chopped onion
1 clove garlic, crushed
1 teaspoon curry powder
½ teaspoon salt
¼ teaspoon chilli powder
2 teaspoons cinnamon
3 cups milk
3 cups cooked pumpkin purée
1½ cups cream
sour cream and chives to garnish

In a large saucepan melt the butter and sauté the onion and garlic until soft. Add the curry powder, salt, chilli powder and cinnamon for one minute. Add the milk, cream and pumpkin purée and heat gently. Pour into a blender or food processor and blend until creamy. Serve warm, or re-heat to the desired temperature without boiling. Garnish with a dollop of sour cream and Thyme Croutons.

Spicy Pumpkin Soup

THYME CROUTONS

3 tablespoons olive oil
3 cups French or thick toast-slice white bread, diced
½ teaspoon freshly ground pepper
½ teaspoon thyme

Preheat the oven to 190 °C (375 °F). In a large oven-proof pan, heat the oil over low heat. Add the bread and toss; season with pepper and thyme, then toss again. Place the pan in the oven and bake for 10–12 minutes until browned. Store in an airtight container for approximately one week.

FESTIVE LASAGNA

500 g / 1 lb. uncooked instant lasagna sheets
1 kg / 2 lb. steak, minced
1 onion, chopped
2 cloves garlic, minced
2 cans (400 g) or 4 cups whole tomatoes, chopped and undrained
1 cup tomato paste
2 teaspoons sugar
2 teaspoons salt
2 teaspoons dried basil
½ teaspoon chilli powder
½ teaspoon ground black pepper
250 g / 8 oz. ricotta cheese
2 large eggs, beaten
½ cup fresh parsley, chopped
1 large bunch spinach leaves, slightly cooked and drained
4 cups mozzarella cheese, grated
1 cup Parmesan cheese, grated

In a frying pan combine the minced steak, onion and garlic and cook until the mince is no longer pink, stirring occasionally. Stir in the tomatoes, tomato paste, sugar, salt, basil, chilli powder and pepper. Reduce heat and simmer for 20 minutes.

In a bowl, blend ricotta, egg and parsley. Spread a thin layer of meat sauce in a large, shallow lasagna dish. Layer one third of the uncooked lasagna on top of that, then half of the spinach leaves, half of the remaining meat sauce, mozzarella and Parmesan cheeses. Repeat the layers, finishing with a layer of lasagna. Spread the top with the ricotta mixture and sprinkle with more grated cheese. Bake in the oven 190 °C (375 °F) until bubbly; approximately 1 hour. Allow to stand for 10 minutes before cutting. Sprinkle with fresh chopped parsley, chives or a selection of fresh herbs.

APPLE CAKE

This cake is versatile, keeps well and is just as suitable served for afternoon tea without the Eggnog Ice cream.

125 g / 4 oz. butter, melted
1 500 g can apple pie filling or equivalent, lightly stewed
1 cup sugar
1 egg
1 ¼ cups flour
2 teaspoons cinnamon
1 ½ teaspoons baking soda
½ cup sultanas

Mix all the ingredients and spoon into a greased 20–23 cm/8–9 in. cake pan or two 20 cm/8 in. pans. Bake at 150 °C (300 °F) for approximately 40–45 minutes (less time when in two pans). Serve warm, sprinkled with icing sugar, with Eggnog Ice Cream.

We are all familiar with Eggnog as a Christmas drink. However, it also makes a thick, rich, creamy ice cream. Apple Cake recipe is overleaf on page 159.

EGGNOG ICE CREAM

2 cups milk
2 cups cream
2 teaspoons vanilla essence
7 large egg yolks
¾ cup sugar
½ teaspoon freshly grated nutmeg
2 tablespoons rum
2 tablespoons brandy
extra nutmeg
1 cup combined glacé fruits, almonds and chocolate, finely chopped

In a large saucepan combine the milk, cream and vanilla essence and bring to the boil. Whisk together the yolks and sugar. Add the cream mixture in a stream while whisking, then transfer the custard to a saucepan. Cook the custard over moderate heat, stirring constantly with a wooden spoon until it coats the back of the spoon. Strain through a fine sieve. Allow the custard to cool and stir in ½ teaspoon nutmeg, brandy and rum, then chill the custard, covered, overnight. Stir in the additional nutmeg and freeze the custard in an ice-cream maker, according to the manufacturer's instructions. Add combined fruit, almonds and chocolate, then freeze until firm.

Apple Cake with Eggnog Ice Cream

HERBED COTTAGE BREAD

3 cups self-raising flour
1 cup cornmeal, finely ground
1 teaspoon baking powder
1 teaspoon dried thyme
1 tablespoon parsley, finely chopped
salt and pepper
¾ -1 cup milk
60 g / 2½ oz. butter, melted

Combine all the dry ingredients with the thyme and parsley. Pour in the milk and mix to a scone-like dough. Pour the melted butter into a small bowl. Divide dough into small portions about the size of a walnut. Roll each ball in the melted butter and place lightly in a greased, round cake pan. Continue until all dough balls have been coated and evenly placed in the pan. Evenly pour over any remaining butter. Bake in a very hot oven 220 °C (450 °F) for 25 minutes or until the top of the loaf is golden brown. Tear into chunks and serve warm.

CHRISTMAS EVE SUPPERS

Herbed Cottage Bread
Oyster and Corn Chowder
Marmalade Glazed Ham
Carrot and Parsnip Tart
Buttered Beans
Christmas Eve Spiced Nut Cake
Garlic Roasted Lamb Cutlets with Cranberry Port Sauce
Chocolate Truffle Loaf with Chocolate Mint Sauce

Herbed Cottage Bread and Oyster and Corn Chowder

A ham provides the basis of the Christmas meal and continues to be an ingredient of many meals during the festive period. Accompanied by salads, or used on chunky, wholemeal bread and mustard sandwiches for picnics, ham is always enjoyable.

OYSTER AND CORN CHOWDER

12 bacon rashers, chopped
1 large red pepper, diced
1 large green pepper, diced
2 onions, chopped
2 tablespoons butter
3 potatoes, peeled and diced
salt and freshly ground pepper
½ teaspoon dried thyme
3 cups drained oysters (canned may be substituted) reserve liquid
3 cups bottled clam juice or good strong fish stock
2 cups cream
2 cups frozen or canned sweetcorn kernels
snipped chives or spring or green onions

Cook the bacon in a large, heavy saucepan over medium heat until the bacon begins to brown. Transfer the bacon to a paper towel. Add the peppers to the saucepan and cook until beginning to soften — about 5 minutes, stirring often. Transfer to another paper towel. Add the onions and butter to the pan. Reduce heat to medium low and cook until onions are tender. Add the potatoes to the pan and season with the salt and pepper. Stir for 2 minutes. Mix in the thyme. Add the reserved oyster juice, clam juice and cream to the pan and simmer until potatoes are tender — 20 minutes. Add the corn, cooked bacon and peppers and simmer for 4 minutes. Add the oysters to the soup. Turn off the heat and allow to stand until the oysters begin to curl — approximately 1–2 minutes. Adjust the seasonings. Ladle soup into bowls and sprinkle with chives.

MARMALADE GLAZED HAM

1 x 6 kg / 12 lb. leg cooked ham

GLAZE
½ cup marmalade
rind of 2 oranges, cut into thin strips
juice of 2 oranges
¼ cup honey
1 tablespoon French mustard
freshly ground pepper to taste

Remove the rind from the ham by running a thumb around the edge of the ham just under the rind. Begin pulling from the widest edge, using your fingers to loosen it from the fat. When the rind is removed to within 10 cm/4 in. from the shank, cut through the rind with a sharp knife. Cut along the fat at 3 cm/1 in. intervals, then cut in the opposite direction to form diamonds. (The knife should cut through the flesh slightly.)

To make the glaze, combine all the ingredients in a small saucepan. Heat until well combined, stirring frequently. Place the ham in a roasting dish and pour over the glaze. Marinate several hours (or overnight in refrigerator) basting occasionally. Bake in a moderate oven 180 °C (350 °C) for 35–40 minutes per kilogram. Baste frequently.

Marmalade Glazed Ham

Carrot and Parsnip Tart

CARROT AND PARSNIP TART

EASY PASTRY SHELL
1 cup flour
3 tablespoons sugar
60 g / 2½ oz. butter
1 large egg yolk

In a food processor combine the flour and sugar. Add the butter cut into small pieces and process until it resembles breadcrumbs. Add the egg yolk and process until the dough holds together when pressed. Press evenly over the bottom and sides of a 20–23 cm/8–9 in. tart pan with a removable bottom. Blind bake at 170 °C (325 °F) for 15–20 minutes. Remove from the oven.

FILLING
2 cups carrots, peeled and grated
2 cups parsnips, peeled and grated
½ cup water
3 large eggs
2 teaspoons grated orange peel
2 tablespoons flour
⅔ cup sugar
1 cup natural unsweetened yoghurt
2 teaspoons lemon juice
salt and pepper to taste

While the tart shell is blind baking, place the carrots, parsnips and water in a frying pan. Bring to the boil over a high heat, then reduce to low. Cover and simmer, stirring occasionally, until the vegetables are soft and the liquid has evaporated. Remove from heat and allow to cool. Whisk the eggs, orange peel, flour, sugar, yoghurt, lemon juice and salt and pepper in a bowl until blended. Stir in the carrots and parsnips. Pour the mixture into the pre-baked tart shell. Bake at 170 °C (325 °F) for about 35–40 minutes or until the centre of the tart is just firm. Allow to cool for 10 minutes (or completely), before running a knife around the edge and removing the tart pan.

❖

CHRISTMAS EVE SPICED NUT CAKE

250 g / 8 oz. butter
1 cup sugar
1 cup brown sugar, firmly packed
1 cup fruit mincemeat
1 cup apricot jam
4 eggs
3 cups flour
¼ cup cocoa
1 teaspoon ground nutmeg
1 teaspoon ground cinnamon
½ teaspoon ground cloves
1 cup natural unsweetened yoghurt
1 teaspoon baking soda
1 cup raisins
1 cup walnuts, chopped
½ cup pecan nuts, chopped
extra nuts for decorating plus ½ cup red and green glacé cherries
Caramel Frosting

Preheat oven to 180°C (350°F). Grease and flour 3 x 23 cm/9 in. sponge pans. Cream butter and both sugars in a large bowl. Stir in the fruit mincemeat, jam and eggs. Mix in the dry ingredients and spices alternately with the yoghurt. Blend well. Stir in the raisins, walnuts and pecans. Pour the batter into the prepared pans. Bake about 45–50 minutes or until the centre springs back when touched. Allow the cakes to cool for 10 minutes in the pans before turning out. Then allow to cool completely. Place one layer on a serving platter and spread the top with the Caramel Frosting. Top with the second layer and spread that with further frosting. Repeat with the remaining layer. Sprinkle with the extra walnuts, pecans and cherries to decorate.

❖

CARAMEL FROSTING

150 g / 5½ oz. butter
1½ cups brown sugar, firmly packed
½ cup milk
1 teaspoon vanilla essence
3 cups icing sugar

Melt the butter in a heavy saucepan. Add the sugar and milk, stirring until the sugar dissolves. Increase heat and bring to the boil. Remove from heat. Allow to stand until lukewarm — 30 minutes. Stir in the vanilla and whisk, adding icing sugar until the mixture is creamy in texture.

This is a deep cake that provides an alternative to the traditional Christmas cake, and it keeps well.

Christmas Eve Spiced Nut Cake with Caramel Frosting

Chocolate Mint Sauce is excellent to have on hand for last-minute desserts, or as an ice cream topping, and is an alternative to Christmas Eve Spiced Nut Cake for this menu.

GARLIC ROASTED LAMB CUTLETS WITH CRANBERRY PORT SAUCE

Allow 4–5 cutlets per person, depending on the size of the cutlets
6 large cloves garlic, crushed
1 cup red wine
2 cups oil
3 tablespoons dried rosemary

Heat this mixture until boiling, stirring constantly. Cool down and strain out the rosemary. Pour over the cutlets and marinate for at least 6 hours. Drain the marinade off the cutlets, then roast in a moderately hot oven. Don't overcook, as the cutlets are best left slightly pink. They can also be precooked and kept warm.

CRANBERRY PORT SAUCE

500 g / 1 lb. fresh cranberries or the equivalent frozen
1 cup port
½ cup red wine and ½ cup water
2 tablespoons sugar
2 tablespoons arrowroot

Boil all the ingredients, with the exception of the arrowroot, for 10 minutes. Strain to remove any pips or skins, then return to the saucepan. Mix the arrowroot with a little water, spoon a little of the cranberry mixture into it, then pour that back into the saucepan, whisking continuously; this avoids a gluey consistency. Whisk until the liquid thickens and clears. Serve immediately. Ladle a spoonful of the sauce onto warmed dinner plates and then arrange the cutlets. Garnish with a small sprig of fresh rosemary.

CHOCOLATE TRUFFLE LOAF WITH CHOCOLATE MINT SAUCE

2 cups cream
3 egg yolks, slightly beaten
500 g / 1 lb. chocolate
½ cup light corn syrup
½ cup unsalted butter
¼ cup icing sugar
1 teaspoon vanilla essence
Chocolate Mint Sauce

Line a loaf pan 23 x 12 cm/10 x 5 in. with plastic wrap. Mix ½ cup cream with the egg yolks. In a saucepan, stir the chocolate, corn syrup and butter over gentle heat until they are melted. Add the egg mixture, stirring constantly. Cook for 3 minutes, then allow to cool. Beat the remaining cream, sugar and vanilla until soft peaks form; fold into the chocolate. Pour into the loaf pan and refrigerate overnight. Serve with Chocolate Mint Sauce.

CHOCOLATE MINT SAUCE

½ cup full cream
250 g / 8 oz. milk or dark chocolate
¼ cup peppermint liqueur or 1 teaspoon peppermint essence

Put the cream into the saucepan and bring to the boil. Break the chocolate into squares and add to the cream. Remove the pan from the heat and stir until the chocolate has melted. When smooth, add the peppermint liqueur and allow to cool, giving an occasional stir; this sauce becomes very thick on standing. Gently re-warm the sauce before use. It may be stored in a wide-necked jar in the refrigerator for up to one month.

Garlic Roasted Lamb Cutlets with Cranberry Port Sauce is an alternative to Marmalade Glazed Ham for this Christmas eve supper menu.

Chocolate Truffle Loaf with Chocolate Mint Sauce (recipe page 166)

CHRISTMAS MORNING FRESH FRUITS IN CHAMPAGNE

1 small white melon
1 punnet strawberries
2 kiwifruit
3 tablespoons kirsch (optional)
½ bottle champagne
fresh mint leaves

Cut the melon in half and scoop out the seeds. Make as many balls as possible using a melon baller, or cut the flesh into cubes. Wash, hull and halve the strawberries. Peel the kiwifruit, halve and slice thinly. Place all the fruit in a bowl and pour over the kirsh. Place in the refrigerator overnight. When ready to serve, arrange the fruit in small glass bowls or champagne goblets and spoon over the liquid. Decorate with the mint leaves. Pop the chilled champagne open and pour it over the fruit to fill the glasses.

CHRISTMAS BRUNCH EGGS WITH CAVIARE

2 tablespoons butter
8 large eggs
4 tablespoons sour cream
cracked black pepper
8 teaspoons caviare
fresh dill to garnish

Carefully take the top quarter of the egg shells off (discard these) and place the eggs in a bowl. Wash the egg shells out very carefully and set aside. Beat the eggs very gently. Melt the butter in a saucepan over a low heat. Add the eggs and stir with a wooden spoon until they are just beginning to set, 3–4 minutes. Remove from heat and stir in the sour cream and cracked pepper. Spoon the scrambled eggs back into the washed egg shells and top with a spoonful of caviare and a sprig of dill.

CHRISTMAS BREAKFAST OR BRUNCH MENU

Christmas Morning Fresh Fruit in Champagne
Christmas Brunch Eggs with Caviare
Bacon Curls
Glazed Cinnamon Buns
Puffed Apple Pancake
Spicy Hot Chocolate

Christmas Brunch Eggs with Caviare and Bacon Curls

BACON CURLS

Allow 2–3 rashers of bacon per person

Remove any rind from the bacon rashers. Cut each rasher into two strips lengthways. Roll up loosely and secure with toothpicks. Grill until cooked and nicely browned.

GLAZED CINNAMON BUNS

DOUGH
3 teaspoons active dried yeast
½ cup warm water
3 tablespoons sugar
2 tablespoons butter
½ cup milk
1 teaspoon salt
1 large egg
3–3¼ cups plain flour

FILLING
1½ tablespoons butter, melted
½ cup brown sugar, firmly packed
2 teaspoons cinnamon
½ cup mixed dried fruit

GLAZE
1¼ cups icing sugar
2 tablespoons butter, melted
2–3 tablespoons milk

To make the dough: In a large bowl mix the yeast and 1 tablespoon of the sugar with ½ cup warm water, leave for 5 minutes or until frothy. Melt the butter in a saucepan, add the milk, the remaining 2 tablespoons of sugar and salt, and heat the mixture until it is lukewarm only. Stir this into the yeast mixture, along with the egg and 3 cups of flour; stir until it forms a dough. Turn onto a lightly floured surface and knead until smooth, using the extra ¼ cup flour if required. Place the dough in an oiled bowl and let it rise until it doubles in bulk — approximately 1 hour. Turn the dough out onto a lightly floured surface again and roll into a rectangle about 1 cm thick.

Brush with the melted butter. Stir together the brown sugar and cinnamon, then sprinkle evenly over the dough. Sprinkle with the dried fruit. Starting with the longest side, roll up the dough tightly, sponge-roll fashion. Cut cross-wise into 12 equal pieces and place in greased, deep muffin pans. Allow the buns to rise covered in a warm place for 45 minutes or until golden.

Make the glaze while the buns are baking. Sift the icing sugar, whisk in the butter and 2 tablespoons of milk until combined. Whisk in the remaining milk to make a thick but pourable glaze. Remove the buns from the oven and turn out of the pans. Pour approximately 1 tablespoon of glaze over each bun. (They can be dusted with icing sugar just before serving.) Makes 12 buns.

PUFFED APPLE PANCAKE

6 large eggs
1 cup milk
⅔ cup flour
½ teaspoon salt
4 large apples, peeled, cored and sliced
4 tablespoons lemon juice
5 tablespoons butter
½ cup brown sugar, lightly packed
1 teaspoon cinnamon
pure maple syrup, warmed to serve

Mix together the eggs, milk, flour and salt. Toss the apple slices with 2 tablespoons of the lemon juice. Melt the butter in a 30 cm/12 in. fluted quiche dish in a preheated oven 210 °C (415 °F). Remove the dish from the oven and lay the apple slices evenly over the bottom. Return to the oven until the butter sizzles; do not let the apples brown. Remove from the oven and immediately pour the batter over the apples. Mix together the brown sugar and cinnamon and sprinkle the mixture over the batter. Put back in the oven for 25–30 minutes then drizzle the remaining 2 tablespoons of lemon juice over the top. Cut into portions and serve immediately with the warm maple syrup as an accompaniment. This is a truly divine dish.

Glazed Cinnamon Buns and Puffed Apple Pancake

Spicy Hot Chocolate. This recipe makes enough for eight people.

SPICY HOT CHOCOLATE

1 cup water
200 g / 8 oz. chocolate, roughly chopped
5 cups milk
3 tablespoons brown sugar
½ cup cream
½ teaspoon cinnamon
pinch nutmeg
8 cinnamon quills

Heat the water, add the chocolate and stir until dissolved. Add the milk and bring slowly to the boil. Stir in the sugar. Lightly whip the cream with the cinnamon and nutmeg. Pour the hot chocolate into eight mugs and top with a dollop of cream. Serve the hot chocolate with a cinnamon quill in each mug to stir in the cream.

CHILLED APRICOT SOUP

125 g / 4 oz. dried apricots
1 cup water
½ cup medium white wine
⅓ cup natural unsweetened yoghurt

Soak the dried apricots in the water for one hour. Place in a saucepan and simmer for 10 minutes. Purée the apricots and cooking liquid in a food processor or blender until smooth. Add the wine and yoghurt; process until combined. Turn into a bowl and chill. Serve with a dollop of yoghurt and fresh herbs or chives to garnish in individual bowls.

CHEESE AND CARAWAY MUFFINS

250 g / 8 oz. flour
4 teaspoons baking powder
125 g / 4 oz. tasty grated cheese
2 tablespoons caraway seeds
¼ cup cooking oil
1 egg
1½–2 cups milk
pinch salt

Mix the sifted flour and baking powder in a large bowl. Add the grated cheese and caraway seeds, then the oil, egg, salt, and enough of the milk to form a dough the consistency of runny porridge; don't overmix as the dough needs to be quite soft so it is pourable. Spoon the mixture into well greased, deep muffin pans. Sprinkle a few shreds of cheese on top of each muffin for a glossy finish. Bake in a hot oven 200 °C (400 °F) for 10–12 minutes, until well risen and golden brown. Makes 12 large muffins or 36 mini cocktail-size muffins.

COUNTRY STYLE PATE

200 g / 7 oz. butter
¼ teaspoon dried thyme
½ teaspoon dried marjoram
1 medium onion, finely chopped
3 cloves garlic, crushed
500 g / 1 lb. chicken livers
½ teaspoon salt
¼ teaspoon nutmeg
2 tablespoons cognac
4 tablespoons port
extra melted butter

In a large saucepan melt the butter, add the herbs and then sauté the onion and garlic until soft. Add the washed and trimmed chicken livers, cooking gently until just done. Do not over-cook. Pour the contents from the saucepan into a food processor or blender, then add all the remaining ingredients except the extra melted butter. Blend until smooth. Pour into one medium-sized pâté bowl or into small individual ones. Have the extra melted butter hot, and carefully separate the clarified butter from the white milk solids underneath. Discard the milk solids and spoon the clarified butter over the top of the pâté to ensure a thin covering. The pâté will look quite soft, but will firm when refrigerated. Serve with crackers, melba toast or chunky pieces of French bread.

PICNIC FOR A WARMER CLIMATE

Chilled Apricot Soup
Cheese and Caraway Muffins
Country Style Pâté
Tropical Reef Marinated Seafood Salad
Red, White and Green Festive Salad
Maple Glazed Ham
Lemon Tassies
Mince Pies

Maple Glazed Ham, Cheese and Caraway Muffins, Chilled Apricot Soup, Country Style Pâté, and Lemon Tassies.

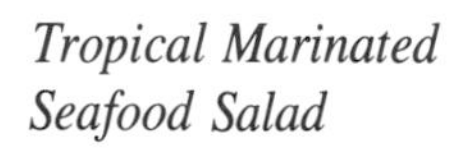

Tropical Marinated Seafood Salad

TROPICAL REEF MARINATED SEAFOOD SALAD

Use dense white fish fillets — orange roughy, snapper, etc.

300 g / 10½ oz white fish fillets, boned and skinned
juice of 3–4 fresh limes
juice of 3–4 fresh lemons
approximately 2 cups coconut milk
½ cup each of the following: lightly poached scallops, smoked mussels, cooked crayfish/lobster, cooked whole prawns, crabmeat
½ cup gherkins, chopped
½ cup red and green pepper, chopped
fine shreds of lemon and lime peel for garnish
fresh dill or mint sprigs

Cut the fish into long thin strips, then cover and toss in the mixed fresh lemon and lime juice. Marinate for at least 2 hours, but overnight is preferable; the fish is 'cooked' when white in colour. Drain the excess juice off the fish and toss in the coconut milk. Add any additional seafood, then stir through the gherkins, red and green pepper, and shreds of lime and lemon peel. Keep well chilled. This can be served in individual clam or scallop shells, or on a bed of salad greens. Garnish with fresh dill or mint sprigs.

RED WHITE AND GREEN FESTIVE SALAD

500 g / 1 lb. green beans, sliced diagonally
1 white melon, peeled and diced
1 200 g can waterchestnuts, drained and sliced
250 g / 8 oz. mushrooms, sliced
24 black pitted olives, drained
500 g / 1 lb. cherry tomatoes, halved
2 jars (approximately 175 g / 6 oz.) marinated artichoke hearts
1 teaspoon fresh basil, finely chopped
1 teaspoon lemon peel, finely grated

Lemon Tassies can be made with any citrus fruit — limes or oranges are delicious alternatives.

2 tablespoons parsley, chopped
2 teaspoons lemon juice
1 cup soya bean oil
garlic salt and pepper

Cook the beans in a saucepan of boiling water until tender yet crisp — 4–7 minutes. Drain and plunge into iced water to cool. Drain again and place in a salad bowl. Add the waterchestnuts, melon, mushrooms, olives and tomatoes to the beans. Drain the artichokes, and add to the bowl. (Halve the artichokes if they are too big). In a small bowl, combine the artichokes, herbs, oil, lemon peel and juice. Whisk lightly and pour over the salad. Season to taste. Cover and refrigerate for 4 hours.

❖

MAPLE GLAZED HAM

3 tablespoons maple syrup
3 tablespoons brown sugar
3 tablespoons prepared mustard (not grainy)

Remove the skin from a fully cooked ham by running a thumb around the edge of the ham just under the rind. Begin pulling from the widest edge, using your fingers to loosen the rind from the fat. Cut the rind off close to the shank. Cut along the fat diagonally in one direction, then in the opposite direction, to form diamonds. Press one clove stud into the centre of each diamond.

Gently heat the glaze ingredients together and spread them over the ham. Heat in the oven at 170 °C (325 °F) for 35–40 minutes until well glazed and heated through.

❖

LEMON TASSIES

1 cup flour
½ cup icing sugar
125 g / 4 oz. butter
3 tablespoons lemon juice
3 tablespoons melted butter
2 large eggs
150 g / 5 oz. sugar
whipped cream for garnish

Place the flour and icing sugar in a food processor. Cut the butter into small pieces and add to the food processor; process until it resembles breadcrumbs and will cling together when pressed.

Preheat the oven to 180 °C (350 °F). Grease the mini muffin pans, pinch off small pieces of the pastry and press into prepared muffin pans. Mix the lemon juice, melted butter, eggs and sugar in a bowl. Divide the filling evenly among the muffin pans. Bake at 180 °C (350 °F) for 20–25 minutes. Remove from the pans while still slightly warm and allow to cool on a wire rack. Serve topped with a dollop of whipped cream. Makes 20.

The Christmas Table

Creamed Chestnut and Sherry Soup
Avocado with Sour Cream, Smoked Salmon and Caviare
Vinaigrette Dressing
Roast Turkey with Cranberry, Apricot and Wild Rice Stuffing
Plum Perfect Goose
Giblet Stock
Potatoes in Goose Fat
Ginger, Pear and Waterchestnut Stuffing
Honey Glazed Ham
Spiced Oranges
Sweet Roast Onions
Brussels Sprouts with Caraway and Almonds
Honey Glazed Parsnip and Carrots
Snowpeas
Bûche Noël
Whipped Chocolate Frosting
Christmas Fudge
White Christmas Candy

The formal Christmas table set with gleaming crystal, silver, crackers, and a beautiful centre-piece of evergreens, lilies, and altar candles.

This soup is an unusual combination of chestnuts and sherry and is a rich, full-flavoured start to the Christmas meal.

❖

CREAMED CHESTNUT AND SHERRY SOUP

8 tablespoons unsalted butter
4 x 250 g / 8 oz. cans whole roasted chestnuts
1 carrot, peeled and sliced
1 parsnip, peeled and sliced
1 cup celery, peeled and finely chopped
8 cups chicken stock
1 cup medium sherry
3 tablespoons parsley, finely chopped
½ teaspoon finely grated nutmeg
salt and freshly ground pepper to taste
2 cups cream
sour cream and cayenne pepper to garnish

Melt 4 tablespoons of butter in a heavy saucepan over a medium heat. Add the chestnuts and sauté until heated through — 5 minutes. Set aside. Melt the remaining butter in a heavy large saucepan over medium heat, add carrot, parsnip and celery and sauté until soft, approximately 10 minutes. Add the stock and bring to the boil. Reduce heat to low, add the chestnuts, sherry, parsley, nutmeg, salt and pepper. Simmer for 15 minutes then purée the soup in batches in a food processor. Transfer to a clean, heavy saucepan, stir in the cream and simmer gently to heat up, stirring frequently. Ladle into bowls, serving each with a dollop of sour cream and a sprinkle of cayenne.

AVOCADO WITH SOUR CREAM, SMOKED SALMON AND CAVIARE

Place half an avocado on a nest of alfalfa sprouts or salad greens. Fill the hollow with sour cream followed by thinly sliced smoked salmon and caviare. Garnish with fresh herbs, parsley or mint sprigs, edible flowers etc. Serve with a Vinaigrette Dressing separately in a small jug.

VINAIGRETTE DRESSING

1 cup light olive oil
⅓ cup white wine vinegar
1 teaspoon prepared French mustard
juice and grated zest of 1 medium lemon
1 clove garlic, crushed
salt and freshly ground black pepper

Place all the ingredients in a blender or food processor, with salt and pepper to taste. Blend on maximum speed for 15–20 seconds. Makes 1½ cups of dressing.

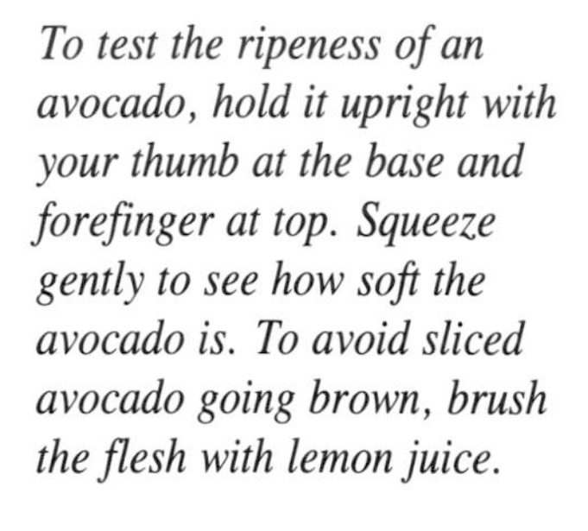

To test the ripeness of an avocado, hold it upright with your thumb at the base and forefinger at top. Squeeze gently to see how soft the avocado is. To avoid sliced avocado going brown, brush the flesh with lemon juice.

Roast Turkey with Cranberry, Apricot and Wild Rice Stuffing.

ROAST TURKEY WITH CRANBERRY, APRICOT AND WILD RICE STUFFING

1 turkey, approximately 6 kg / 12 lb. in weight
30 g / 1½ oz. butter, melted
1 tablespoon soya bean oil

STUFFING: Enough to fill the above turkey —
3 cups fresh white breadcrumbs
2 cups wild rice, cooked and drained
½ cup dried apricots, chopped
½ cup cranberry sauce
½ cup blanched almonds, sliced
1 medium-sized onion, finely chopped
rind and juice of 1 lemon
3 tablespoons parsley, finely chopped
1 large egg, beaten
½ teaspoon mixed dried herbs
salt and freshly ground pepper to taste

Thaw the turkey thoroughly before proceeding. Wash and dry the inside and outside of the bird. Weigh and calculate the cooking time at 30–35 minutes per kilogram/15–20 minutes per pound.

To prepare the stuffing, combine all ingredients well. Spoon the prepared stuffing into the cavity of the turkey. Cover with neck flap and secure with skewers. Secure the wing tips to the body and tie the legs together. Place the turkey in a large roasting dish and brush with melted butter and oil combined. Pour about 4 cm/1¼ in. water into the dish. Brush a large piece of foil with a little butter and oil before covering the turkey loosely, but ensuring a tight seal around the rim of the dish. Roast the turkey in a very hot oven for 3½ hours approximately for a 6 kg bird. Remove the foil for the last 30 minutes' cooking, to allow browning. To test if the turkey is cooked, insert a skewer into the thigh. If juices run clear, the turkey is cooked; if they are still pink, continue cooking a little longer.

PLUM PERFECT GOOSE

1 x 5.5 kg / 11 lb. goose
3 onions
1 orange
1 teaspoon salt
freshly ground pepper
600 ml / 1 pint goose giblet stock
2 cups white wine
ground cinnamon and allspice
2 cups dark plum jam
3 tablespoons red wine vinegar
3 tablespoons soya bean oil

To make the plum sauce, place the jam in the top part of a double boiler and add red wine vinegar plus the rind of 1 orange and ½ teaspoon ground cinnamon. Place over barely simmering water and heat gently, stirring occasionally until the jam is warm and runny. Push through a fine sieve, then gradually beat in 3 tablespoons oil. Add salt and pepper to taste. Place in a covered container and refrigerate. This can be made up to a week ahead.

Have the goose at room temperature. Wipe the bird inside and outside. Peel the onions and quarter them. Quarter the orange without peeling it. Place both inside the cavity of the goose and secure the flaps at both ends with skewers. Prick the skin of the goose all over with a fork. Mix together 1 teaspoon salt, freshly ground pepper and ¼ teaspoon of cinnamon and allspice: rub this mixture over the skin of the goose. Calculate the roasting time at 20 minutes per 500 g/1 lb. Sit the goose in the roasting pan breast side up and cook at 220 °C (425 °F) for 20 minutes. Pour off the accumulated fat, then reduce heat to 180 °C (350 °F) for the remaining time, pouring off fat as necessary. Reserve fat for roasting the potatoes. Turn the goose once or twice during roasting. Check the goose is cooked by piercing its thigh, to see if the juices run clear. If they are still pink, continue cooking until done.

Plum Perfect Goose is the alternative provided in this menu to Roast Turkey.

Extra stuffing can be cooked separately in patty pans, served as individual portions and layered around the side of the turkey or goose, as illustrated on page 180.

Ginger, Pear, and Waterchestnut Stuffing is an alternative recipe for turkey stuffing, and the Honey Glazed Ham is an alternative to either turkey or goose.

GIBLET STOCK

1 tablespoon fat reserved from goose
goose neck, heart, gizzard
1 onion, roughly chopped
1 carrot, chopped
4 cups chicken stock
freshly ground pepper to taste

Heat the oil in a heavy saucepan over medium heat. Add the goose neck, gizzard and heart. Sauté until golden brown — 6 minutes. Add the onion and carrot and sauté 5 minutes. Add the stock and pepper and bring to the boil. Reduce heat and simmer 1 hour. Skim the fat from the surface of the stock, then strain the stock through a sieve into a bowl.

POTATOES ROASTED IN GOOSE FAT

1½ kg / 3 lb. potatoes, peeled and cut into chunks
2 cups reserved goose fat from roast goose
salt and freshly ground pepper

Place the potatoes in a large pot of cold salted water. Bring to the boil. Reduce heat and simmer until the outside of the potatoes are tender, yet a knife will not pierce the centre. Drain. Run the fork tines across the surface of the potatoes to score. Preheat the oven to 200 °C (400 °F). Pour the goose fat into a large roasting pan, add the potatoes and turn to coat. Roast until golden brown and very tender — 30 minutes — basting occasionally. Transfer to paper towels, using a slotted spoon and allow to drain. Season and serve.

GINGER, PEAR AND WATERCHESTNUT STUFFING

3 tablespoons butter
1 large onion, coarsely chopped
3 cups fresh white breadcrumbs
2 large cans pear halves, drained and diced
1 200 g can waterchestnuts, drained and diced
½ cup raisins
3 tablespoons crystallised ginger, finely chopped
2 tablespoons cider vinegar
1 teaspoon ground ginger
pinch salt

In a large saucepan melt the butter, add the onion and sauté until golden. Remove from the heat and stir in the breadcrumbs, diced pears, sliced waterchestnuts, raisins, crystallised ginger, cider vinegar, ground ginger and salt. Mix thoroughly and stuff inside the cavity of the turkey. Cook as usual for a roast turkey.

HONEY GLAZED HAM

3 tablespoons honey
3 tablespoons brown sugar
3 tablespoons prepared mustard (not grainy)

Remove the skin from the fully cooked ham by running a thumb around the edge of the ham just under the rind. Start pulling from the widest edge using your fingers to help lift the rind away from the fat. When it is removed as far as the shank, cut through the rind with a sharp knife. Score the ham at intervals to form diamonds and stick a whole clove stud into each diamond.

Heat all the glaze ingredients together and spread over the ham. Bake in the oven 170 °C (325 °F) for 35–40 minutes.

Sweet Roast Onions and Potatoes Roasted in Goose Fat

SWEET ROAST ONIONS

Cut the onions in half, leaving the skins on. Place them cut side down in a roasting pan with thin layers of goose or turkey fat. Roast for 35–40 minutes in a hot oven until cooked. The onions naturally caramelise with their own sweetness.

SPICED ORANGES

12 mandarins or small oranges
2 cinnamon quills
2 whole cloves
4 cups water
4 cups sugar
½ cup orange-flavoured liqueur, e.g. Cointreau or Grand Marnier

With a vegetable peeler remove two long strips of peel from two of the oranges. Place in a clean 1 litre/2 pint jar, or divide between two smaller jars. Completely peel all 12 oranges, removing as much of the white pith as possible, and pierce each one in several places with a fork. Pack into the jars. Add the cinnamon quills and cloves. In the saucepan, bring to boil the water and sugar. Reduce the heat to low and simmer uncovered for 10 minutes or until syrupy. Remove from the heat and add liqueur. Pour over oranges, cover and allow to cool. Refrigerate until ready to serve.

Spiced Oranges

BRUSSELS SPROUTS WITH CARAWAY AND ALMONDS

3 tablespoons butter, softened
1 teaspoon caraway seeds, chopped
salt and pepper to taste
1 kg / 2 lb. brussels sprouts, trimmed and a cross cut into the base of each sprout
1 cup blanched almonds, toasted

In a bowl, blend the butter, caraway seeds and salt and pepper to taste. Steam the brussels sprouts for 12–15 minutes or until they are tender, then toss them in the bowl with the butter and caraway seeds. Add the almonds and stir gently through.

If almonds are not your favourite, try hazelnuts, which are equally delicious.

Brussels Sprouts with Caraway and Almonds.

HONEY GLAZED PARSNIPS AND CARROTS

500 g / 1 lb. parsnips
500 g / 1 lb. carrots
40 g / 1½ oz. butter
2 tablespoons honey

Peel the carrots and parsnips, discarding the tops and tips. Cut into finger-length sticks. Boil or steam until just tender. Drain. Return to the saucepan, add butter and honey and stir over a medium heat until well mixed. Serve immediately.

SNOWPEAS

Carefully trim the ends of the snowpeas. Blanch by immersing in scalding water, drain, and toss in cream, salt, finely ground black pepper, and finely chopped basil or mint. This recipe is also nice with freshly shelled peas. Cook gently for a few minutes with a knob of butter and a pinch of brown sugar, then drain the water. Add the cream and herbs. Allow the cream to warm through and serve.

Honey Glazed Parsnips and Carrots.

TRADITIONAL CHRISTMAS PUDDING

375 g / 12 oz. raisins
375 g / 12 oz. sultanas
250 g / 8 oz. currants
185 g / 6 oz. prunes, chopped
185 g / 6 oz. mixed peel, chopped
1 tablespoon grated lemon rind
90 g / 3 oz. blanched almonds, chopped
1 carrot, grated
250 g / 8 oz. fresh white breadcrumbs
1 cup sugar
1 cup flour
½ teaspoon salt
2 teaspoons mixed spice
4 large eggs
¾ cup milk
1 cup brandy
250 g / 8 oz. butter, melted

Grease a 2 litre/8 cup pudding basin. Mix together the raisins, sultanas, currants, prunes, mixed peel, lemon rind, almonds, carrot, breadcrumbs and sugar. Sift the flour with the salt and spices, then add to the fruit mixture. Lightly beat the eggs, then add the milk, brandy and melted butter. Stir into the dry ingredients and fruit and mix well. Fill the prepared basin, leaving a 25 mm/1 in. space at the top. Cover with greaseproof paper and tie securely with string. Cook in a large pot of boiling water which comes three quarters of the way up the sides of the basin. Replace the lid of the pot and boil gently for 5 hours; top up with boiling water as necessary. Remove the basin and cool. On the day of serving, reheat the pudding by boiling in the same manner for 2 hours.

HARD SAUCE

Beat 150 g/5 oz. butter to soften. Gradually beat in 1½ cups of sifted icing sugar; continue beating until light and fluffy. Stir in ¼ cup brandy and ¼ cup cream. Spoon into a bowl, cover and refrigerate.

BUCHE NOEL

3 large eggs
100 g / 3½ oz. castor sugar
75 g / 3 oz. plain flour
2 tablespoons cocoa
1 tablespoon water

Grease and line a sponge roll pan. Dust with flour. Whisk the eggs and castor sugar until very thick and light in colour. Sift the flour and cocoa directly over the egg mixture and fold in carefully, to avoid knocking air out of the mixture. Fold in the tablespoon of water. Pour into the prepared pan and level off the surface. Bake at 200 °C (400 °F) for approximately 12 minutes: the sponge should have shrunk slightly away from the sides. Loosen the edges of the sponge from the pan and turn out onto a large sheet of greaseproof paper sprinkled with castor sugar. Gently roll up with the greaseproof paper and set aside to cool. (Greaseproof paper should be rolled inside with the sponge.) When cool, unroll the sponge, discard the greaseproof paper then spread with Whipped Chocolate Frosting. Reroll the sponge. Cover the whole sponge with thc rcmaining frosting. Decorate by running the tines of a fork along length so that it resembles a log of wood. Dust finely with icing sugar before serving.

Bûche Noël
The Bûche Noël is traditionally made as an edible version of the yule-log.

❖

WHIPPED CHOCOLATE FROSTING

150 g / 5½ oz. butter
1½ cups brown sugar, firmly packed
½ cup milk
1 teaspoon vanilla essence
3 cups icing sugar
4 tablespoons cocoa

Melt the butter in a heavy saucepan. Add the brown sugar and milk, stirring until the sugar dissolves. Increase heat and bring to the boil, then remove from the heat and add the cocoa and icing sugar. Allow to stand until lukewarm — 30 minutes. Stir in vanilla and then whip, adding icing sugar gradually until the mixture is smooth and creamy.

Bûche Noël

CHRISTMAS FUDGE

300 g / 10½ oz. marshmallows
100 g / 3½ oz. butter
1 tablespoon water
200 g / 7 oz. dark chocolate, chopped
1 teaspoon vanilla essence
1 cup pecan nuts, chopped

Line a 23 cm/8–9 in. square pan with tinfoil. In a medium saucepan, melt the marshmallows, butter and water. Stir in the chocolate, vanilla and nuts. Stir until well mixed and the chocolate has melted. Pour into the prepared pan and refrigerate. Cut into pieces when completely cold.

WHITE CHRISTMAS CANDY

2½ cups rice bubbles
1 cup coconut
¾ cup icing sugar, sifted
1 cup full cream milk powder
1 cup mixed dried fruit and red and green glacé cherries
250 g / 8 oz. solid vegetable shortening, melted

Combine all the dry ingredients in a large mixing bowl and stir in the vegetable shortening. Mix well. Press the mixture into a greased 30 cm x 20 cm / 12 in. x 8 in. sponge roll pan. Refrigerate overnight. Serve cut into squares or cut out into Christmas shapes with cookie cutters.

These are fabulous as edible Christmas gifts. Or, if you are a guest for Christmas dinner, let your host know you will be providing the treat to go with coffee.

Christmas Fudge and White Christmas Candy

This cool dessert is an alternative to the heavier, traditional puddings. A lighter, fruit version is often appreciated by guests who have over-indulged in the previous courses.

CHRISTMAS FRUIT COMPOTE

125 g / 4 oz. raisins
125 g / 4 oz. sultanas
60 g / 2½ oz. currants
125 g / 4 oz. pitted prunes
125 g / 4 oz. dried apricots
2 crisp green apples, peeled, cored and thinly sliced into rings
juice and grated rind of 1 orange
juice and grated rind of 1 lemon
¼ teaspoon each ground cinnamon, allspice and ginger
60 g / 2½ oz. brown sugar
water
½ cup brandy
125 g / 4 oz. blanched almonds, toasted

Place raisins, sultanas, currants, prunes, apricots, apple, orange and lemon rinds and juices, spices and brown sugar in a saucepan. Add water just to cover, stir to mix and bring to the boil. Remove from heat and stir in the brandy. Transfer to a bowl and leave to cool. Cover and refrigerate for two days, to allow flavours to develop. Sprinkle with toasted almonds and serve with lightly whipped cream, vanilla ice cream or a light custard.

Christmas Fruit Compote

Food from Cassell's Household Guide *circa 1880.*
TOP CENTRE: Turkey garnished with flowers.
TOP LEFT: Sandwiches.
TOP RIGHT: Tongue.
CENTRE LEFT: Open Jelly with whipped cream.
CENTRE: Centre stand for fruit and flowers, Custards in tray.
CENTRE RIGHT: Jelly of two colours.
BOTTOM LEFT: Game Pie. Aspic Jelly in dish.
BOTTOM RIGHT: Lobster.
BOTTOM MIDDLE: Ham.

IMAGES OF CHRISTMAS PAST

MacW

'A Winter Song' from The Graphic, *Christmas number, 1883. This lithograph shows the Robin Redbreast in full Christmas song.*

'The Fruits of the Christmas Tree'
Come, tell me, if you're able,
To name a vegetable,
Of all that bud and shoot,
Which yields such charming fruit.

In such variety,
As such children's Christmas Tree!
Let June display her cherries,
Her rasp — and her strawberries;

Let glowing August come,
Laden with pear and plum;
December conquers both,
With his luxuriant growth.

The Graphic, *Christmas, 1874.*

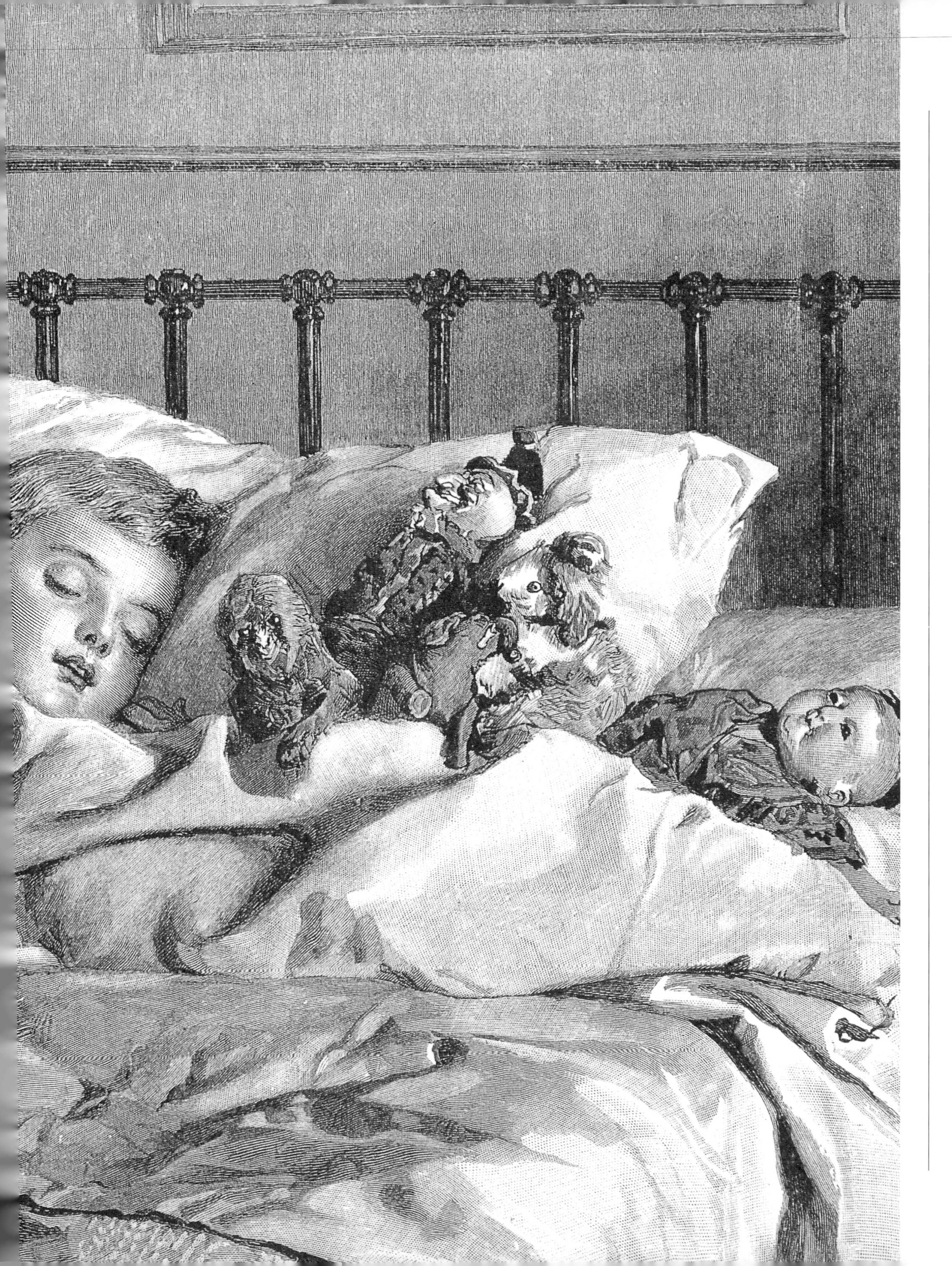

'Father Christmas's Annual Visit: Some Strange but Welcome Bedfellows'
The Graphic, *Christmas, 1862.*

'Here Comes Santa Claus!' from The Illustrated London News, *Christmas, 1891.*

'The Christmas Hymn' from The Illustrated London News, *Christmas, 1890.*

'The Mistletoe Gatherer' from The Graphic *Christmas, 1876.*

'Under The Mistletoe'
The Illustrated London News.

'Under The Mistletoe: A Little Sister' from The Illustrated London News – *1891.*

'Blind Man's Buff — ''I know who you are'' '. A very popular Victorian parlour game as portrayed in The Graphic, *Christmas, 1871.*

'Christmas in Canada — Amateur Carol Singing at Longueil on the St. Lawrence'. The Graphic, *Christmas, 1876.*

'Choosing his Christmas Turkey — The March Past' The Graphic, *Christmas, 1875.*

'Dancing in the New Year — A welcome to 1873'.
The Graphic, *1873.*

Sydney-based author **Lynn Bryan** was born in the United Kingdom and arrived in New Zealand as a teenager. Lynn trained as a journalist and has worked as a feature writer on newspapers and magazines (including the *Listener*) for the past 20 years. Lynn was more recently the deputy editor of *MORE* and the editor of the *MORE Design Book.*

Jo Seagar trained at the Cordon Bleu School in London and spent many years in Europe gaining a wide knowledge of the food and wine industry. She recently sold 'Harley's', the restaurant she established in Auckland upon her return from Europe, to devote more time to her food styling and consultancy business and to her work as a regular columnist with *North and South.*

Designer **Donna Hoyle** is known internationally for her unique ranges of coordinated paper products. Donna works across many design disciplines and has more recently turned her talents to book design, winning the design and production section of the New Zealand Book Awards for her work on *Focus on New Zealand.*

Stylist **Craig Thorburn** has worked extensively in display for the past two decades, the last four years as designer for the retail store, The Christmas Heirloom Company. Recently Craig started his own company, Grand Illusions, but still finds time for his special interest in antiques and restoring his home to its original spendour.

Photographer **John Pettitt** has enjoyed a varied career as a freelance photographer, including a period with the BBC in the United Kingdom, and an assignment in the sub-Antarctic. He has a particular interest in design and fine cuisine. His recent published work includes the award-winning *Huka Lodge's Cook Book* which was produced in collaboration with Donna Hoyle.

Fionna Hill trained as a florist at the Constance Spry Flower School in London. Having gained her diploma, Fionna worked for Constance Spry shops in Chelsea and Mayfair, and has decorated, among numerous other places, Covent Garden, Westminster Abbey, St Margaret's Chapel, the Royal Opera House and Madame Tussaud's Waxworks, plus society weddings and exclusive homes. Fionna now lives and works in Auckland.

INDEX

RECIPES